LET THE CASH FLOW

Let the Cash Flow

A practical guide to getting
paid on time by your customers

Simon J. Littlewood

Mark Laudi

© 2021 Marshall Cavendish International (Asia) Pte Ltd

Published in 2021 by Marshall Cavendish Business
An imprint of Marshall Cavendish International

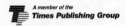
A member of the
Times Publishing Group

Other Marshall Cavendish Offices:
Marshall Cavendish Corporation, 800 Westchester Ave, Suite N-641, Rye Brook, NY 10573, USA • Marshall Cavendish International (Thailand) Co Ltd, 253 Asoke, 16th Floor, Sukhumvit 21 Road, Klongtoey Nua, Waṭṭana, Bangkok 10110, Thailand • Marshall Cavendish (Malaysia) Sdn Bhd, Times Subang, Lot 46, Subang Hi-Tech Industrial Park, Batu Tiga, 40000 Shah Alam, Selangor Darul Ehsan, Malaysia

Marshall Cavendish is a registered trademark of Times Publishing Limited

National Library Board, Singapore Cataloguing in Publication Data
Names: Littlewood, Simon J. (Consultant). | Laudi, Mark, author.
Title: Let the Cash Flow: A practical guide to getting paid on time by your customers / Simon J. Littlewood, Mark Laudi.
Description: Singapore : Marshall Cavendish Business, 2021.
Identifiers: OCN 1243202700 | ISBN 978-981-4928-29-8 (Print paperback)
Subjects: LCSH: Accounts receivable. | Collecting of accounts. | Business enterprises–Finance.
Classification: DDC 658.15244–dc23

Printed in Singapore

Ad Maiorem Dei Gloriam

For Leslie P. Shaw

Revenue is vanity
Profit is sanity
Cash is reality

– Anonymous

Contents

Why we wrote this book

When I first sat down with Simon over coffee to talk to him about accounts receivable, collections and cash flow, my training business was going strong.

It was 2016. Our sales were growing. Our customer base was growing. But our overdraft was growing, too. Some months we were struggling to pay salaries and rent. We were spending a growing amount of time chasing overdue invoices. The sales wheels were spinning, but cash flow was bogged down.

How could this be, I often wondered, when we had a delightful list of blue-chip clients.

How could this be, when we had a wonderfully warm working relationship with the decision makers who booked our services?

How could this be, when bookings were rolling in and I was virtually working 24/7?

Some months before my fateful coffee with Simon, I had made yet another collections call during which the customer told me she couldn't find the invoice … oh wait, there it was, at the bottom of her in-tray.

I was fed up. I rolled up my sleeves and conceived of an online platform to send automated email reminders to our clients, telling them in the nicest possible way to pay up!

"A customer who doesn't pay isn't a customer, it's a charity," I ranted to Simon, and underscored it with a final swig of my cup. "Or worse, a parasite!"

He chuckled and shook his head, and uttered those words that at first I hated to hear. "Mark, when you don't get paid on time, it's because of something you did or did not do *before* your invoice became due."

How could this be? A customer doesn't pay, and it's *my* fault?

But I contemplated this for a while. Simon was very experienced in this area, had a 30-year track record in consulting to large companies, was a working capital specialist. Could he be right?

One of the most uncomfortable realisations about not getting paid on time was that most of the time it *was* my own fault: Invoices not sent in hard copy. Invoices not sent. Invoices not even written. Not checking the invoice for errors. Not checking whether the invoice had arrived. Not confirming the invoice was going to be settled by the due date. Not aware of the customer's lengthy and elaborate onboarding process before delivering the product or service. I couldn't even submit the invoice, whether it was correct or not.

Not only have I come around to Simon's way of thinking, there is a pressing need to spread the word. You would think something as essential as cash flow would get a great deal of attention. But we have found the issue doesn't even get enough recognition from the companies that need it most: Small and Medium Enterprises.

Just look at the shambolic invoices you receive from time to time from some of your suppliers. Misspelling your company name. Misstated prices. Missing Purchase Order. Missing account details to remit payment to. Missing due date. On occasion, I have even seen an expiry date on invoices! So, I just need to wait it out and then I won't need to pay it, is that right?

Many SMEs string along their own suppliers as long as possible before they promise to send a cheque and then take weeks more before they actually do, yet expect customers to pay instantly. And then they assume that after providing the product or service they are somehow magically going to get paid. And if not, shrug, there's nothing they can do about it.

The working capital gap starts with this knowledge gap. Worse, a whole industry has sprung up to take advantage of it. Invoice factoring services, microlending services, invoice gateways, payment gateways, procurement portals, accounting software and yes, automated reminder email platforms such as the one I had myself conceived, all promise to help you improve cash flow.

But what they are all missing is that getting paid on time is not a *technology* problem. It's a *communications* problem. It follows that it requires a communications solution.

That's what this book is about: how to talk to your customers so you are not only getting paid on time but building your relationship with them in the process.

Some of it will make you uncomfortable, as it challenges the entrenched notion that a delayed payment is always the customer's fault.

But as you settle back and read it with your own cup of coffee in hand, you will feel empowered because there *is* something you can do. You will feel reassured because you can regain control of your balance sheet. You will feel your business move forward because cash flow will gain traction when you rev up sales. You will look forward to calling customers as a contribution to customer service, rather than a drain of your valuable time.

And you will never have to make those dreaded collections calls again.

Part 1
This book, and how to use it

1.1 What's in this book

This book is designed to help you get paid on time by your customers. It is intended for companies of all sizes who allow their customers credit terms and are struggling with late payments.

Whether you are a start-up or a substantial enterprise, you will find here a solution to the problem of managing accounts receivable.

We simply argue that, since solvent companies always pay some suppliers every month, you should make it your objective to be one of the suppliers who gets paid.

This requires removing any real or imagined obstacle to timely customer payment through a single-minded approach to communication and service.

If you currently get paid in cash and are not owed money by any customers, you might want to spend your time – and your money – elsewhere. Unless you are just curious – in which case, read on!

Nor is this a manual for those in crisis, though we certainly offer good advice for companies for whom late payment has become critical, as well as a "quick wins" guide in Part 8.

Every company which offers credit terms will benefit from what is in this book, because the solution offered builds better customer relationships, unites your team, and creates resilience in times of disruption.

In the book we lay out practical steps to becoming "first in line to get paid" based on the adoption of what we call the Virtuous Revenue Cycle, which emphasises customer intimacy and service.

Early on, we describe and debunk nine commonly held misconceptions about why companies (you!) get paid late, to help you build alignment within your own team by anticipating objections.

Overview
We recommend you read this book as a whole, but to help you get started there follows a summary of what is in each of the 9 parts.

Part 1: Definitions
In Part 1 we define "accounts receivable" (AR), or simply, "receivables". We describe how the money your customers owe you can be broken down into a "terms-driven" and a "process-driven" component, each of which must be treated differently.

We also suggest you measure AR using the term Days Sales Outstanding (DSO) so you can track how effectively you are managing this important asset. We provide examples of DSO measures.

Part 2: The Virtuous Revenue Cycle (VRC)
In Part 2 we introduce the Virtuous Revenue Cycle (VRC) and briefly summarise each of its elements.

The VRC is a cycle of continuous improvement which changes service culture, delights customers by anticipating and responding to their every need and ensures that you get paid on time.

The magic of the VRC is that the delivery of prompt payment is an implicit outcome rather than an explicit one – your customer interactions begin and end with service and intimacy, and ugly conversations about tardy payments are consigned to the past.

The VRC begins with top-down ownership and a clear definition of mutual expectations through written credit policy and uses proactive customer service and responsiveness and total team engagement to identify and resolve unmet customer expectations and assure timely payment.

Your VRC will also, over time, provide your team with new and important skills, and enable greater competitiveness and growth.

Part 3: Case studies
This book distils years of hands-on experience, including some successes and many failures. To encourage you to follow the VRC path, we include three examples of companies which followed these principles under our guidance.

One was already a substantial recently listed technology MNC destined to grow into a $5bn company; the second, a $20m B2B SME now transitioning out of SME status (>$100m); and the third, a small start-up now doubling in size each year.

Each one has seen enormous success – including rapid growth, strong cash flow, and remarkable resilience during disruption.

Each one acknowledges in the clearest terms how adopting the principles in this book early on has played a key role in their success, with some compelling examples.

In one case, the co-founder of a specialty chemicals SME describes how rapidly improving receivables management became a life-or-death issue – and how solving that issue using the VRC built a very healthy and cash-rich company over time.

Part 4: Into action

In this part each component of the Virtuous Revenue Cycle is introduced in detail, with clear steps, illustrations, and Do's and Don'ts.

The content of this part should be treated as a whole – without every element of the VRC, your programme will either not succeed or after brief success will fail to endure.

Part 5: Other opportunities

Once you have the VRC in place and working, other things become possible because of the enhanced quality of your processes, the reduction of customer risk, and the improved transparency of receivables data.

Your data on discrepancies and the financial and service benefits to your customer of root-cause elimination will permit you, in selected cases, to negotiate terms-reduction with customers.

We lay out a simple but effective methodology for you to use to identify and agree terms reduction with selected customers.

We also explore the opportunity to leverage credit insurance to offset bad-debt risk, summarising interviews with leaders in this field.

In addition, we address the significant opportunity which now exists to leverage digital communication in the service of customer engagement at selected stages of the VRC.

Part 6: Your start-up advantage

Most start-ups fail. Most often they fail by running out of cash. A start-up that takes this book seriously and follows its suggestions from the very outset will enjoy a distinct advantage and will have mitigated the principal failure risk.

Established companies which have operated in a certain way for years and have a defined culture face greater obstacles when they try to install the VRC and assure timely payment.

They already have complex operations, staff used to behaving in a particular way (and in many cases being rewarded for it), as well as customers who have become used to paying late. Their journey will be a much tougher one and they will need to make greater efforts to correct things.

If you can, ensure you build the Virtuous Revenue Cycle into your start-up culture from day one and do not simply assume that you can easily deal with it later.

To help start-ups, we provide a simplified checklist with links to the various parts of this book that provide greater detail.

Part 7: How to make it happen

Data shows that 70% of major change programmes fall short of their objectives. Many companies grapple ineffectively with their receivables challenges, and some make multiple vain attempts to change payment outcomes.

Part 7 therefore equips you for success by providing guidelines for building the case for change, tracking the pace of change and areas of internal resistance, and creating internal consensus. We also suggest the best sequence to use when installing the VRC in your company.

We also suggest using "outcome-based training", a type of training that incorporates real business situations from day one and builds hands-on skills.

Part 8: Postscript

We emphasise again that fixing receivables should not be treated as a one-off. You cannot make a few changes and then move on. If you do, the problem will quickly resurface!

This is a programme of continual action to bring about a cultural change that delivers happy and loyal customers, healthy cash flow, and the ability of your team to learn and improve.

Part 9: Appendices

We include a glossary of terms, useful templates we have assembled that may be helpful to you as you build your VRC, and other relevant resources.

1.2 Definition and measurement of Accounts Receivable

Accounts receivable, or receivables for short, or AR (both definitions appear in this book) consist of invoices which have been produced for goods or services that you have already provided to your customer but which have not yet been paid.

Receivables can be measured purely in value – as in "We have US$10.3m of receivables."

This is not enough. We advocate measures that relate receivables (what we are owed) to what we have sold (sales), either measuring receivables as a percentage of sales, or in "Days of Sales Outstanding" or DSO.

DSO is our recommended measure.

If you allow your customer credit terms, then when you total your receivables, some will be "current" – not yet due for payment based on the agreed credit terms for that customer – and some will be "overdue" – i.e. should already have been paid given the terms that were agreed at the beginning of the transaction.

Definition and significance of DSO

If you are selling on credit terms, then the more sales you have, the greater will be the total value of your receivables.

In one sense, therefore, growing receivables are a measure of your success and a healthy outcome of growth. Receivables may grow even if your customers always pay you on time, simply because you are invoicing more.

For this reason, tracking receivables value alone is not helpful as a way of measuring how good you are at getting paid on time. Since that is the subject of this book, we are going to suggest you use DSO as it is a better measure of the effectiveness of your receivables management effort.

Days Sales Outstanding (DSO) tracks total receivables in days of sales equivalent.

If my sales in a 30-day month are $10m, and I have $10m in receivables, then my DSO is 30 – that is, equivalent in value to 30 days of sales.

Fig. 1.1 - DAYS SALES OUTSTANDING (DSO) FORMULA

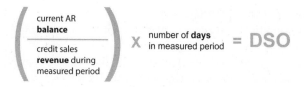

$$\left(\frac{\text{current AR balance}}{\text{credit sales revenue during measured period}} \right) \times \frac{\text{number of days}}{\text{in measured period}} = \text{DSO}$$

Several ways of measuring DSO

There are different ways of measuring DSO, and each has its advantages and disadvantages.

At this point we simply want to encourage the idea that the best sales-related measure of how well you manage your receivables is DSO and we strongly suggest you adopt it as a key measure of how well you are doing with this programme.

Your DSO *is* within your control

Often when companies struggle to get paid on time, they attribute that failure to external forces beyond their direct control, such as the market or the customer (see 2.2: Challenge receivables myths).

We believe strongly that the key to getting paid on time lies in your own hands, whatever you may have been told or may be hearing from your colleagues, customers or lenders.

To get paid on time, you need to think about receivables as a measure of the effectiveness of your own processes, starting from how you act when you first onboard a new customer to the time their payment arrives in your bank account.

We advocate using DSO because, by relating receivables to sales, DSO provides a normalised measure of how well you are managing getting paid on time.

DSO tells you how effective your processes are. DSO also provides a firm basis for internal comparison, so that you can see how your receivables performance is improving or worsening month by month, irrespective of whether your sales go up or down.

DSO also allows a common basis for external comparisons – you can benchmark yourself against competitors or other similar businesses.

If your business is growing in a healthy way, the value of your receivables may increase. But your DSO (time it takes to get paid) can go up or down, depending on what *you* do to influence it.

When DSO goes up, that generally tells you that you are taking longer to get paid because of something you should have done differently, and that you may therefore need to change something.

It is a key message of this book that *you* determine your DSO and can take firm control, if you choose to.

DSO consists of two distinct parts

If you grant credit to customers, then you will always have outstanding receivables.

If you allow your customers 30 days credit, then you will have a DSO of at least 30 even if all your customers pay you on time.

In the real world, not all customers pay on time, some pay late. Your DSO at any one time will consist of a part driven by the terms you grant – in this case 30 days – and another part caused by delayed customer payments, the overdue part.

If you have credit terms of 30 days but your DSO is 40, then we would say that 30 days of your DSO is "terms-driven" and 10 days is "process-driven" because the latter is in your control and your customer should have paid you so that you have a DSO of 30.

Since you probably have multiple customers with different terms, calculating the "terms-driven" part of your DSO requires adopting a weighted average measure which tracks the blend of terms you are using every month (see BPDSO).

DSO will always grow, untended

In a busy business, growing healthily with new customers, DSO *never stays the same*. Unless you actively manage all aspects of your receivables, and have an effective VRC, your DSO is more likely to increase than to decrease.

There are many reasons why DSO tends to grow, but here are four common ones:

1. Customers like their cash, and will delay if you let them

Customers (even good customers) look for ways to pay later – and if you do not ask promptly for payment, you are giving them a way to pay later.

They say to themselves, in effect: "We have not been specifically asked for a payment by this supplier, so apparently it is not very important to them when they get paid." (The second case study alludes to such a case.)

Remember that even well-meaning customers tend to draw out their payments over time unless they are actively managed. This is not reprehensible in their eyes. They regard it as acceptable business practice.

They may take advantage of lapses on your part, including the rationalisation that if you do not ask maybe you do not especially care, but in their own minds they are simply playing the game in a logical way.

Fig. 1.2 -
POOR TERMS DISCIPLINE & PROCESS VARIABILITY
LEAD TO RECEIVABLES INCREASE

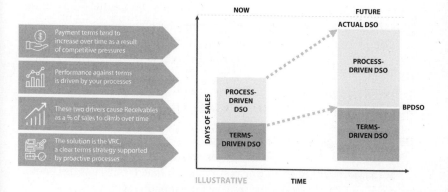

2. Salesmen (and women) are primarily motivated to sell

One thing that may cause DSO to grow is the tendency of a sales team to allow longer payment terms when asked by a prospective customer.

They may see this flexibility as a way of pleasing the customer and improving the odds of closing a sale. A keen salesman wants the sale and if he does not appreciate the financial impact of slower payment he may feel it is perfectly fine to grant more days to pay.

And a customer will nearly always ask! If you say yes, he will ask again!

Later, we will equip your sales team with an understanding of why the payment terms they agree to matter very much. We will help them find new ways to get the sale whilst staying firm on terms.

For now, let us note that this is a natural occurrence in a growing concern without active receivables management, and one you will need to address.

3. Shift to export? Beware

When companies grow outside their home turf, into other countries, they encounter new challenges. Other countries have different customs and often different business terminologies.

These days, in our connected world, most export customers demand credit terms – in the past, letters of credit were almost universally used. Insisting on LOC is now often a competitive disadvantage.

The fact is that export business tends to result in more complexity for you to manage, and the potential for slower payment.

Getting more export sales is a good thing, but again, unmanaged, will tend to grow your DSO.

4. The perils of complexity

The fourth reason DSO grows is business complexity. Unless you have a really good VRC, increasing complexity – which generally comes with growth – will in itself result in a lengthening of DSO.

Complexity can include the number of customers, new points of sale, the number of products, the number of different terms, currencies, banks, fiscal rules, etc.

We all seek growth. Complexity, unmanaged, tends to favour the customer who wants to hang on to his money because it is harder for you to manage.

DSO does not go down, unmanaged

DSO will nearly always go up unless you actively manage it.

Managed, it will go down, and our promise is that if you follow this book, your DSO will decrease significantly in a few months.

But it never stays still, so if you do want to have more cash and a lower DSO in the future, you have no choice but to act now and to introduce changes that are designed to last.

BPDSO: Best Possible DSO

In practice, few companies have a single credit term. They tend to have a range of different customer payment terms, and often these proliferate as the business grows and becomes more complex.

Large customers with many operations are often adept at progressively obtaining longer terms over time. Once you have granted one of their subsidiaries or affiliates longer terms – perhaps to win new revenue – you are likely to be asked to extend the longer term to all of their operations.

To track the impact of granting longer terms, you will need to measure the terms-driven part of your DSO – which gets more complicated as you grow. We encourage you to use something called BPDSO: best-possible DSO.

This involves calculating a weighted average theoretical BPDSO by noting what percentage of your sales are made on each credit term and calculating a weighted average.

The benefit of calculating BPDSO is that you can track whether, due to a change in business mix (i.e. more sales to customers with longer terms) or to sales choices, your weighted average terms are going up.

This would mean that your DSO would have increased even if all your customers had paid you to terms, which of course they never do.

Here is an example:

Fig.1.3 - HOW TO CALCULATE BPDSO

	Credit Term	Number of Days	Sales Per Term ($m)	Sales Per Term as % of Total Sales	Term BPDSO	
Term 1						Number of Days * % of Total Sales /100
Term 2						
Term 3						
Term 4						
Term 5						
Term 6						
Term 7						
Term 8						
		TOTAL SALES		BPDSO		Sum of Term BPDSO

Because we believe – and will show – that late payments occur for the most part because of something you could have done differently, we refer to the overdue portion of your DSO as being process-driven.

Don't worry if this seems strange to you – we will explain in this book how you can get control of late payments by making changes to the way you work with your customers, from the very beginning of the relationship.

Our focus is on helping you to ensure that the overdue portion of your receivables is kept to an absolute minimum.

As we have seen, your actual DSO can go up even if you are paid on time, if you allow customers, on average, longer terms.

So later on (Part 5.1), we explain how it is important to track the terms you grant, using BPDSO snapshots, and how once your VRC is working well you will be able to find ways to reduce BPDSO or average terms. But do not worry about this for now.

In the next section, we dwell briefly on why how well you manage this part of your business is so important.

1.3 Why receivables matter

A lack of sufficient working capital to run your business day to day is by far the biggest cause of business failure. Rarely is it caused by a lack of growth opportunity.

Entrepreneurs are good at creating products and good at selling them. They tend to neglect getting paid on time, often until it is too late. This is the main reason many start-ups fail (see Part 6 for help with your start-up).

By the way, the fact that running out of cash is the biggest cause of company failure holds true, worldwide, for companies both large and small.

This book is concerned with the management of accounts receivable, a term we defined earlier.

Receivables is an area where many companies struggle but where improvement can be achieved relatively quickly if the right changes are made in the right way.

There may also be opportunities for companies to generate cash by reducing stocks of raw materials, work in progress, or finished goods. (You may want to look at these areas but they are not the subject of this book).

Lack of focus
Entrepreneurs, full of zeal and armed with new and differentiated business ideas, are often ill-equipped to handle the impact of their own success on their working capital.

Unless it is consciously and diligently managed, working capital will always go up.

They wrongly believe that with more sales must come more cash. Yet most of the time, for most businesses, growth will require *more* working capital, not less. (See the case studies in Part 3 for examples.)

This predicament is summed up in Figure 1.4 "Margaret makes chairs" which sets out in very simple terms why a vibrant and growing business may need more working capital as it grows and unless it plans for this may find itself unable to meet its commitments.

Fig. 1.4 - MARGARET MAKES CHAIRS

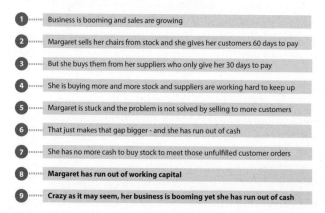

1 ········ Business is booming and sales are growing

2 ········ Margaret sells her chairs from stock and she gives her customers 60 days to pay

3 ········ But she buys them from her suppliers who only give her 30 days to pay

4 ········ She is buying more and more stock and suppliers are working hard to keep up

5 ········ Margaret is stuck and the problem is not solved by selling to more customers

6 ········ That just makes that gap bigger - and she has run out of cash

7 ········ She has no more cash to buy stock to meet those unfilled customer orders

8 ········ **Margaret has run out of working capital**

9 ········ **Crazy as it may seem, her business is booming yet she has run out of cash**

Yet despite its importance, receivables management often suffers a low status within companies, measured by the time invested by management, the relative seniority of those charged with assuring good receivables performance, and their relative remuneration and perceived status.

Business impact of overdue receivables

In a recent survey 66% of business leaders cited cash flow as their primary concern (after the length of the COVID downturn).

Fig. 1.5 - TOP OF MIND

What are the top three most pressing concerns for your company's executive management team?

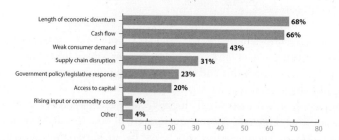

Length of economic downturn	68%
Cash flow	66%
Weak consumer demand	43%
Supply chain disruption	31%
Government policy/legislative response	23%
Access to capital	20%
Rising input or commodity costs	4%
Other	4%

0   10   20   30   40   50   60   70   80

Multiple responses allowed | Source: Mar 26 - Apr 2 CFP survey of 333 finance executives, "The Economy in Limbo"

When you have a high level of overdue receivables, you are being deprived of much-needed cash and you may also be funding borrowing costs to plug the gap.

But the commercial impacts of overdue receivables go well beyond simply creating a cash and funding gap.

Increased costs for you (and for your customer)

You get paid late because your processes allow it. Going to and fro with the customer whilst you resolve discrepancies costs him, and you, money.

You can actually measure the impact of incurring increased operating costs from receivables management and show how, the later the receivable, the greater the investment of time and effort. These costs can include:

- Service time reaching out to the customer
- Travel costs visiting the customer
- Time of other functions invested in resolving discrepancies
- IT costs of producing a correction
- Recurring costs of repeating the same mistake
- Loss of sales time for selling

Remember that, crucially, every time you reach out to the customer to deal with late payment and end up investigating and correcting a discrepancy, it affects your Total Cost to Serve and it is costing the customer money as well.

Later on, when you start to get better at correcting errors before they occur, we will help you demonstrate to your customer how you have saved them money by taking out rework and improving the overall process.

This is important because it will make you an easier and less costly supplier to do business with, thereby increasing the likelihood that you will be able to retain and grow your customers. Because you will have the data to show them how you are cheaper to do business with.

Increasing customer satisfaction

When a well-organised company – say one of your big customers – evaluates a supplier, they will certainly always look at price, product quality and delivery responsiveness.

The best ones, though, also make a point of calculating Total Cost to Serve, which includes looking at a particular supplier (i.e. you) to see how many errors occur on average per transaction, how long it takes you to correct them and how much this adds to their total supplier cost.

It is quite likely that if you are getting paid late, your total supplier cost for your customer is unnecessarily high, because late payments invariably indicate additional rework. A savvy customer will take this additional cost into consideration when deciding which supplier to work with.

When you adopt the VRC and start to systematically identify and eliminate discrepancies, you will have an opportunity to demonstrate to your valued customer how you are saving them money because you care and are improving service quality. You can measure this in terms of time invested and transaction costs.

When your customer evaluates and compares suppliers in order to select the best, you do not want to be considered "high cost". This book will show you how to ensure you are not.

High-cost suppliers (are you one?) have poorer customer retention than low-cost suppliers. That is, if you are getting paid late, you are costing your customer more time and money than your competitor who gets paid on time, and when he works that out, your customer may decide to go elsewhere. Your objective is to be a low-cost supplier and to make your customer aware of that!

Sales productivity

There is another significant implication of having higher than average over-dues compared to your competitors.

Because later payment implies more discrepancies and ensuing corrections, companies with higher DSOs than their competitors tend to be generating more discrepancies and investing more time in correcting them.

Those same companies, when they measure sales and service time using activity-based analysis (ABA), find that significant sales and other time is invested in resolving customer discrepancies.

Interestingly, when we tested this by carrying out a survey, we also found that leadership commonly underestimated the time their sales team spent on dealing with receivables issues with customers.

Fig. 1.6 - HOW WELL DO YOU KNOW THE PERFORMANCE OF YOUR SALES TEAM?

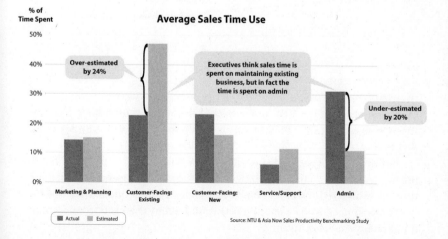

Source: NTU & Asia Now Sales Productivity Benchmarking Study

We show you how to do this measurement in Part 7, as it is a useful way both to highlight the problem and to show sales how the VRC will make their jobs easier by reducing rework.

Sales time spent dealing with invoicing and payment issues is sales time that cannot be spent on selling. Discrepancies therefore also have a negative effect on growth, by depriving your commercial team of much-needed selling time.

When you improve your receivables processes using the VRC, errors will disappear, excuses for late payment will vanish, and your sales and service teams will have more time to spend with the customer growing the business. As opposed to batting away service problems.

When you measure lost sales time, you can also calculate the lost revenue that can result by reversing new sales into existing customer-facing sales time.

Remember: the higher your overdues, the less efficient your receivables management, the less sales time your salesmen have for selling, the greater the lost revenue. Less sales time also means poorer customer service.

Fig. 1.7 - HIGHER DSO CORRELATES CLOSELY TO LOST SALES TIME

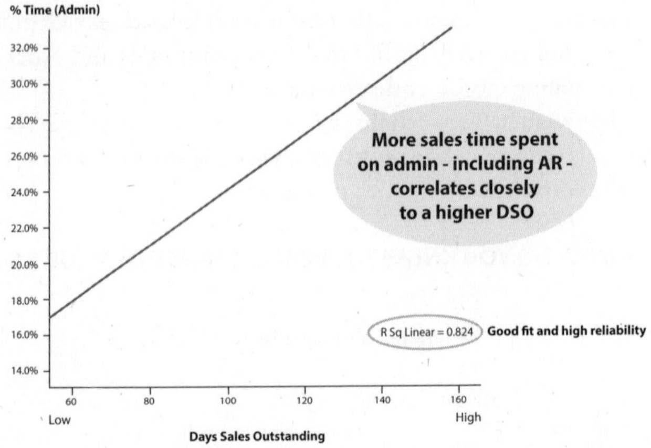

More sales time spent on admin - including AR - correlates closely to a higher DSO

R Sq Linear = 0.824 Good fit and high reliability

Investing in the future
Once you have got the VRC in place and have reduced discrepancy occurrence, your sales team will be largely freed up from receivables and process discussions.

But when you are actually installing the VRC for the first time and clearing up past errors, your sales team will for a short period spend *more* of their time on resolving discrepancies and other issues than they have been used to.

You will need to be clear about this and about the need to make this investment in a better future.

Fig. 1.8 - SALES TIME USED FOR ADDRESSING CUSTOMER RECEIVABLES ISSUES - HOW IT VARIES OVER TIME

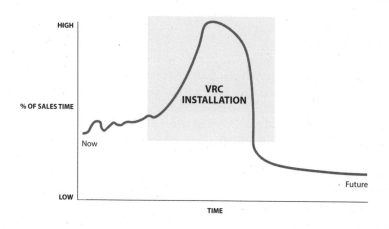

Summary

Receivables matter because when poorly managed they increase operating costs, impact borrowing, limit cash available for investment, damage customer retention, and constrain the effectiveness of your sales team.

In general, companies that have higher DSOs than their peers can be shown to have:

- Less cash to operate and grow
- Higher borrowing
- Less happy customers
- Less happy service and sales staff
- Less productive sales staff
- Higher transaction costs

Later on, we will show how you can measure and track all of these critical performance areas as they improve. We will also provide you with related templates and guides in Part 9.

When building a case for change with your team – see Part 7 – showing how much late payments really cost you by demonstrating all of these impacts may prove critical in gaining their attention and support.

This is why we urge you to investigate these areas and build a detailed case for change before asking your own team to make changes to the ways they think and operate.

1.4 Why receivables matter now

The debt overhang

Many companies, especially SMEs, have taken advantage of cheap and plentiful borrowing to neglect AR discipline over many years, and have allowed overdues to grow to historically high levels.

The availability of cheap borrowing has come about as a result of government policy, principally in the USA and Europe, which has led to the Federal Reserve and the European Central Bank pursuing a policy of quantitative easing (QE).

QE simply means making more and more money available to banks and businesses at historically low interest rates. That money, originally intended to prop up banks, has in fact led to an over-supply of credit. The abundant cash has flowed around the world into equities and real estate, but especially into commercial borrowing.

Companies that in the past would not qualify for corporate debt have been able to raise money very cheaply, and non-traditional intermediaries have been promoting loans to companies of all sizes, including SMEs. In addition (see Fig 1.9), the quality of those loans has progressively eroded.

Fig. 1.9 - HOW HAS CORPORATE DEBT FARED RELATIVE TO GDP GROWTH?

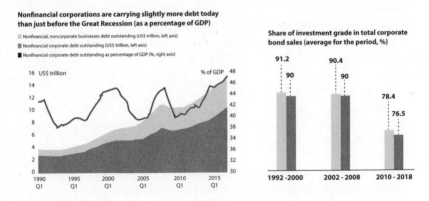

"Why go through the pain of dealing with tricky customer issues when we can simply borrow more cheap money to plug the gap?" is the thinking of many companies under cash flow pressure.

This response to a growing DSO and increasing late payments may seem to offer a quick way of sidestepping internal and customer conflict and focusing instead on growth, but it is unsustainable and toxic.

Not only does it lead you into greater debt, it allows you to ignore the service and relationship gaps that invariably lie behind overdue payments.

Reduced resilience

If you maximise borrowing during normal times to offset weaknesses in your balance sheet which could have been avoided by better management of cash flow, you may find that when real disruptions occur your options have become much more limited.

Companies with this mindset are often poorly positioned to cope with external disruptions to business activity.

In the recent past, disruptions have included:

- Geological and meteorological events
- Geopolitical rivalries
- Trade disputes, which reduce activity and shift supply chains
- Diseases such as SARS or COVID-19, which hinder or prevent commercial activity
- Political instability

When the competitive environment worsens due to these and other factors, many companies naturally try to strengthen customer payment discipline, especially if they are already bumping against borrowing limits.

But in times when everyone is under cash flow pressure, this is a difficult undertaking.

One reason it is difficult is that they will be doing it at the same time as their competitors who are experiencing the same challenges.

They need a differentiated approach, which we call *being first in line to get paid*. This book is that approach.

1.5 How this book will help

This book contains workable solutions to getting paid on time, based on building what we call the Virtuous Revenue Cycle (VRC).

Three very different companies that took our advice and adopted the VRC are included as case studies in Part 3.

In these pages we suggest you make changes to your processes from the very beginning of each customer relationship and will lay each change out in detail in Parts 2, 4 and 5, whilst helpful templates and examples can be found in Part 9.

We are not here to tell you how to close the stable door after the horse has bolted by, for example, employing lawyers or debt collectors. By then it is already too late.

We are not here to tell you how to borrow money from banks or other intermediaries to plug your cash gap. There are plenty of sources for such advice, because there is lots of cash around.

The idea is that by getting paid on time, every time, your need for lawyers, reactive solutions or more borrowing will be reduced.

We have dedicated a chapter to helping you deal with customers who are insolvent and cannot pay (bad debt) because this happens to every company sooner or later.

But we want to help ensure that you *never* get to that situation. Most of the changes we advocate to prevent late payment or bad debt actually occur very early in your customer interactions, not later on when it is already too late to affect outcomes.

The prescription given here is tried and tested. Properly executed, it has helped companies of all sizes to be first in line to get paid.

Because the execution is key – it is easy to make mistakes – we have devoted Part 7 to:

- How to build consensus around the need for change
- How to sequence the changes correctly
- How to check for misalignment or anxiety in your team

This way, you can address misunderstandings and fear promptly and effectively.

Getting paid on time does not depend on automation, on your relative market share, or on your willingness to be aggressive with customers. We address these and other myths in Part 2.2.

Our solution

The key to sustained AR improvement lies in your ability to deliver competitive service and to build – and maintain – customer intimacy.

This intimacy starts early in each relationship. It is based on early and repeated customer contact. It is driven by an internal culture of balance sheet awareness and ownership which starts from the very top, and by clear, consistent communication, as well as rapid responses to errors or omissions, however trivial, wherever found and however identified.

These chapters are based on more than 30 years of working with companies of all sizes across many geographies and industries.

We offer you a high-impact yet easy-to-read how-to guide to de-risking your accounts receivable, accelerating inward cash, and taking your customer service to the next level.

1.6 In disruption be bold

By using a new service-based approach to understand your customers better, you can reduce risk and find new ways to grow and prosper.

Fig. 1.10 - WHAT CAN WE LEARN FROM THE PAST?

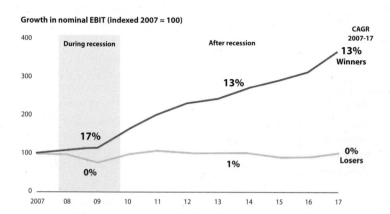

As a reminder that swift action pays dividends, Fig 1.10 show how 13% of listed companies fared well after the 2007 crisis by acting quickly on costs and working capital.

We urge you to be one of them.

This book is mainly about how building genuine intimacy with customers enables longer-term relationships and puts you at the front of the queue when it comes to getting paid.

When you take noise, cost and conflict out of your customer relationship and replace them with the Virtuous Revenue Cycle, you become, over time, easier and cheaper to do business with, compared with your competitors.

We challenge the received opinion that automation, outsourcing, and above all using digital means to transact business is the way forward.

None of these innovations, whilst undoubtedly beneficial if done right, directly addresses the problem of getting paid on time. If you have limited bandwidth, pursuing them may also divert you from the VRC, which is your solution.

One of the things about the customer intimacy that lies behind effective receivables management is that by embracing this new model you will not only be first in line to get paid but will also:

- Improve customer retention by becoming an attentive and low-maintenance supplier
- Free up your sales department from transactions and discrepancies and create bandwidth for
  - Intelligence-gathering to help anticipate risk
  - Building new relationships and investing in existing ones

If you can follow these few principles and build them into your relationship DNA, you have a bulwark against disruption.

You can anticipate disruption early, address it openly, and you can rely on VRC-driven trust and intimacy to put you ahead of your competitors when payment is at issue.

Far from making relationships problematic, a readiness to listen and negotiate during general market stress allows "moments of truth" and great steps forward in retention and trust.

To weather disruption, we encourage you to:

- Pause and ensure you understand your customer's situation properly
- Conduct a customer triage based upon their relative risk and importance
- Identify shaky customers who may be at risk of insolvency, reach out to them, limit the downside
- For the top 20% of customers (consider future growth potential), move quickly to adopt the proactive service model laid out in these chapters, seek to offer support early and often
- Enhance your customer early-warning system – traditional credit reports are generally too reactive to be effective in a real crisis (see Part 2.5: Take risk seriously).
- Coach your sales team on intelligence-gathering – what should they look for when visiting a customer, how can they enhance sharing with competitors
- Talk to competitors – you might be surprised how open they are to sharing when the chips are down
- Hoard your cash as much as you can

This book does not set out specifically to provide a model for accelerating growth, although we will help you measure the impact of enhanced service on the retention of existing customers and freeing up sales time for growth.

Ways to find growth
One common result of disruption is that supply chains change, sometimes dramatically. In other words, customers become more open to moving to new suppliers.

In Asia in late 2019, a trade war between the US and China, followed within months by a China lockdown to arrest the spread of the COVID-19 pandemic, shifted production and supply from China to other countries. Companies struggled to adjust, some doing better than others.

By building greater intimacy with key customers through the VRC, you will find ways to anticipate their challenges, protect your cash flow, and in some cases support them in ways that will redefine your relationship and assure greater growth in the future.

Other (potential) customers who are currently buying from your competitors may come under pressure and be more open to switching some (or all) of their supply – your sales team can be mobilised to listen for these opportunities and taught how to probe for details.

In conclusion, we strongly believe that adopting the service-based solutions in this book so that you build a self-sustaining VRC will make your business more resilient in times of disruption as well as providing you with a more reliable cash flow and a reduced need for borrowing.

Do

- Prepare for disruption by hoarding your cash, both from receivables and elsewhere.
- Have a back-up supply plan especially for the top 20% of inputs and customers.
- Use disruption to cement existing relationships by being the supplier who always listens and responds.
- Upskill your sales team so that existing relationships are strengthened.
- Engage your sales team in active risk assessment and intelligence-gathering so you can detect early when a customer is in trouble, and act to help, or mitigate bad-debt risk (move to cash terms, develop a payment plan, etc.).
- Use your enhanced service model to embrace key accounts, remove obstacles to timely payment and listen for opportunities to grow through adjacencies.

Do not

- Make hasty decisions on accepting higher risk or longer credit simply to get a sale.
- Be seduced into unnecessary borrowing when you can generate the cash you need from getting your invoices paid quicker.
- Extend longer payment terms unless you are certain that customers are solvent.
- Be persuaded that automation will accelerate cash in – automation may well help you reduce transaction costs and even headcount, but the key to getting paid always lies in relationships.

Part 2
The Virtuous Revenue Cycle

2.1 Meet the VRC

Getting paid on time is mainly about relationships and service, and requires that you refine and adopt what we call the Virtuous Revenue Cycle (VRC). It is most especially *not* about vigorously chasing already late payments by any means possible including lawyers, courts and bailiffs.

Fig. 2.1 - MEET THE VIRTUOUS REVENUE CYCLE

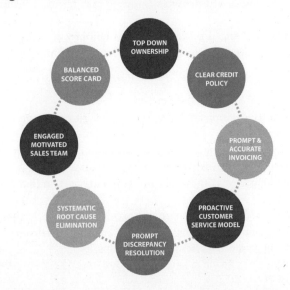

The VRC recognises that building customer intimacy is a constant endeavour, requiring a transparent and self-correcting culture of continuous service and improvement, with

- Active ownership from the very top
- Clear payment and service expectations communicated from the beginning of every customer relationship
- Accurate and timely transactions, including crystal-clear revenue recognition
- Carefully maintained processes of customer intimacy with early identification of issues and their prompt resolution
- Cross-functional engagement linked to service and receivables metrics and variable remuneration

Customer intimacy is not a mysterious bond forged by gifted leaders and salesmen with unique talents. It involves your whole team. It is cultural in nature. It starts at the top and is created by process, hard work and discipline. It takes time to develop, and it is built upon a bedrock of professionalism, openness and service.

The key elements are neatly captured in the Virtuous Revenue Cycle:

The graphic shows the individual activities required to earn customer trust and loyalty and ensure the timely, error-free completion of every transaction.

This book takes each step in the VRC and describes why you need it, what it requires, and how to go about building it.

It can be hard to do

Many companies recognise the need for a change in service culture but struggle to make it happen. Many companies have called on us after one or several internal efforts to change service and payment culture have failed.

Part 7 offers some advice – born of trial and error over many years – on how best to go about making these essential changes so they last and become part of your culture.

These include clearly defining the financial consequences of "doing nothing" and ensuring that the payment impacts of reactive service and discrepancies are measured so as to make clear that the solution lies within, not outside, your own operations.

We urge you to read Part 7. If you rush ahead with implementing your VRC without reading the "how to do it" and "how to avoid common pitfalls" you may find you quickly run into internal opposition, cause customer alarm, and come to a halt.

It is much harder to make this programme work if you go about it in haste, run into trouble, and have to start again! Each time you try to do it, you further erode credibility.

The elements of the VRC
Here is a brief description of each step in the VRC. These steps are explained in more detail in Part 4.

Top-down ownership
A close friend recently reminded me – based on his own experience – how frustrating it is to try and implement any change in company process and culture that is not fully embraced, and led, from the top.

See the case studies in Part 3 for compelling examples of how three leaders, from very different industries and cultures, led a move to the VRC in their companies and thereby laid the foundations for profitable growth with a healthy cash flow.

Each of them stresses the importance of their very direct and visible (senior) ownership of the VRC and how their personal examples changed team culture and gave a new importance to getting paid.

Clear credit policy
In order have a clear understanding of expectations with a customer – without which service and payment performance cannot be tracked or evaluated – every customer should sign a short credit policy that summarises:
- Service expectations on both sides
- Payment terms
- Dealing with discrepancies when they arise
- Key people and contact details
- Timing for future review of the credit policy or of selected elements

Prompt and accurate invoicing
A high percentage of late payments arise from invoice errors. These may include details like price, PO, etc., but they may also be caused by disagreements over when revenue can actually be recognised and an invoice raised. This is a critical issue with companies that deliver a mix of hardware and service (see our first case study in 3.2) where sending an invoice may require that specific acceptance criteria be met, and where those criteria are unclear or not accepted.

Proactive customer service model
Most companies only ask for invoices to be paid when they are already late. Even if you have clear direction from the top, and a signed credit policy with each customer, you can be certain that you will sometimes be paid late if you omit to reach out to your customers until due date has passed.

"You didn't ask so we assumed it was not important" is commonly heard from customers at the outset of a VRC programme.

We therefore advocate introducing a process of early customer contact, immediately after invoicing, to reinforce your commitment to service and demonstrate a willingness to address gaps and issues and resolve them promptly. We call this proactive service.

Unless an issue preventing payment is identified well before invoice due date, it cannot be resolved in time to unblock payment.

In effect, by waiting to ask, you reinforce a customer culture of "I have an issue but since they have not asked for payment I am comfortable waiting to be contacted".

Prompt discrepancy resolution

Often when you contact a customer, he will report a discrepancy. This may be an omission, an error, or simply a dubious attempt to find a reason to delay (like "We cannot find your invoice").

By calling early – soon after invoicing – you identify these "unaddressed expectations" and give yourself the time to resolve them.

But since different issues will have different functional owners, you also need to be clear about who in your organisation must resolve each type of issue and have a service level agreement (SLA) to which you can hold your team.

Systematic root cause elimination

Once you start recording all the discrepancies reported by your customers, you are in a strong position to resolve them and unblock invoice payment.

But you can actually do a lot more to effect lasting change in the ability of your customer to pay you late. We say "ability" because customers feel able to withhold payment if there is a mistake or an omission on your part. Sometimes these "delay enablers" can seem quite trivial!

The more information about discrepancies you are able to collect, the more data you will have on why invoices get held up. When you list the value of invoices held up for payment by each type of discrepancy (the LRF – lost revenue factor), you will discover that 20% of issue types hold up 80% of invoices by value.

When you go back and understand why these top 20% of discrepancies occur, you can work cross-functionally to resolve them at source – so they stop happening.

This may involve clearer communication, paperwork or messaging, or actual changes in process and data, with training.

Engaged, motivated sales team

Just as the company leadership, from the very top, must embrace the VRC and support a two-way service promise, so must all functional leads, and most especially, sales and commercial managers and staff.

If salesmen and women, who probably spend more time with the customer than anyone else, do not understand why there needs to be a clear set of policies and why they are important, and cannot support them and deal civilly and effectively with objections, the VRC will not succeed.

In Part 4 we break this down in more detail, setting out the need for sales training and role-play, and eventually, and most important, a variable remuneration programme (a.k.a. bonus, incentive, etc.) which ties sales personnel to payment and service outcomes financially.

Balanced scorecard

Very often in business, different functions measure success in different ways. An obvious example is that a sales account manager may be measured and rewarded on sales dollars or sales volume whereas the customer service or finance team may be measured on whether the invoice is paid on time or DSO.

There are many other examples of this kind but to get a really effective VRC that lasts, you must create measures of success that tie everybody to the same set of outcomes.

Later on we will look at getting more consistency in the way we measure our team.

Lack of clarity, or ambiguity, from functional leaders who are measured on different – sometimes conflicting – outcomes, will send mixed messages across your entire company and therefore to customers.

Ambiguity always creates opportunities for your customers to exploit these different messages to extend payment delays.

Own your cycle

We encourage you to make your own version of the Virtuous Revenue Cycle, with the active engagement of your leadership team.

By encouraging them to participate, and by developing a jointly owned framework with the right language (terms that you all recognise), both the level of ownership and your probability of success are greatly enhanced.

We have come across many variants, and we think getting the principles right and executing effectively matter a lot more than what you call things.

But before you can do this, you should take care to get your team onside.

Top-down ownership of working capital, including receivables, is essential if you want to build and operate a profitable company which speaks to happy customers with one voice.

That's why this sits at the top – 12 o'clock – of our VRC.

Without committed, cross-functional ownership, you may get short-term improvement in customer payments, but long-term AR stability will be elusive.

Our aim in this book is to help you achieve a long-term cultural change in the way you and your team think of receivables and in the way that you manage them – from an uncomfortable, adversarial process to a win-win programme of service and trust-building.

We call the elements of effective revenue management the Virtuous Revenue Cycle because properly brought to life the VRC is healthy and self-correcting, creates lasting bonds with customers, and produces positive business outcomes.

A salutary example

I spoke to a C-level executive recently who was under cash flow pressure and wanted to solve the issue of late customer payments.

Her instruction to me was: "Go and talk to my receivables people and sort things out. I have a business to grow."

She regarded slow payments as an annoyance and as someone else's responsibility.

I knew right then that I would probably find a frustrated collections team trying to tackle overdues with little senior or cross-functional support, or indeed interest. Sure enough, I did.

Steps

1. Take the Virtuous Revenue Cycle and share it with your leadership team.
2. Carefully consider each element and adapt as you follow the steps in this book, changing the language to suit your business and situation.
3. Take a binary view of each element. Once agreed, policy and action are not up for debate and exceptions are only permitted after very careful scrutiny *and* formal sign-off.
4. Make the VRC part of your culture, communicate it to staff, include progress in company reviews, and have fun with an "elevator pitch".
5. Ensure that it is okay for any team member to talk about customer dissatisfaction or internal dysfunction. Without a healthy honesty and the corrective processes that follow, the discovery of an opportunity to improve is squandered.
6. Be clear that since there are some important changes to make, your team will need to invest time and not take shortcuts, and that it is okay to ask if things are not clear.

Your organisation, afterwards

As your organisation adopts the VRC, there will be a new professionalism. We describe the positive changes you can expect in Part 6. We also include a table to introduce some of the major transitions you will experience.

Do

- Get senior management aligned around the importance of timely customer payment based upon clearly agreed terms of trade.

- Make sure all functional leads and senior managers understand working capital impacts at the conceptual level and are clear about the negative impacts of late customer payment on profitability, cash flow and share price.
- If required, put the leadership through a "balance sheet matters" seminar, with clear takeaways for each of them. Later on, extend this training to team members.
- As a team, develop your own version of the Virtuous Revenue Cycle – setting out the key components of your approach to AR – and share it widely, using it as the basis of internal communication.
- Build awareness of this new culture by having everyone who interacts with customers learn an "elevator pitch" and make it their own.
- With your team, draft a credit policy (see Part 4, with additional templates in Part 9) that clearly states the importance of timely payment and lays out how this will be achieved, step by step, based upon the chapters of this book.
- Get into the habit of encouraging team feedback on customer or internal service issues. You can use an anonymous suggestion box if you like but ideally you want your team to be comfortable speaking openly about opportunities to improve.

Do not
- Make dramatic changes to remuneration, job roles or processes without building the case for change and getting leadership alignment.
- Communicate the need for change in such a way that experienced salesmen, or others, feel implicitly criticised or worry that they will be asked to do things they are unfamiliar with.
- Communicate anything to customers until your entire team is comfortable with the changed focus and has the "language" to promote its advantages both internally and externally (including an elevator pitch).
- Allow customer or internal issues to remain undisclosed, and unaddressed, because of the need to save face, avoid embarrassment, or simply keep the peace – these learnings are pure gold.
- Try to improve receivables levels by abruptly shortening your payment terms. Your focus should first be on clarifying and reinforcing the payment terms you already have in place, using the steps defined in this book to help customers pay you based on those terms.

2.2 Challenge receivables myths

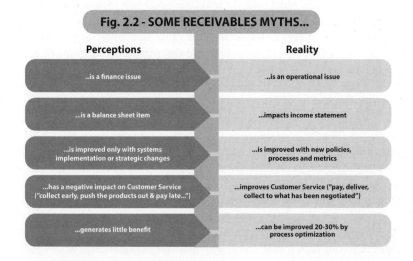

Fig. 2.2 - SOME RECEIVABLES MYTHS...

Perceptions	Reality
...is a finance issue	...is an operational issue
...is a balance sheet item	...impacts income statement
...is improved only with systems implementation or strategic changes	...is improved with new policies, processes and metrics
...has a negative impact on Customer Service ("collect early, push the products out & pay late...")	...improves Customer Service ("pay, deliver, collect to what has been negotiated")
...generates little benefit	...can be improved 20-30% by process optimization

Getting paid is often an afterthought

In many successful and fast-growing companies, getting paid on time is an afterthought and gets little attention until after it has become a problem.

Receivables play second fiddle to creating the product, and marketing, selling and delivering it.

We do understand that these are all very important activities without which no business can be successful.

And for those who carry them out with great professionalism and success, they may very well seem far more compelling than receivables.

But by themselves they are not enough. Because if you do not get paid, you do not have a business, you have a charity.

No matter how clever and compelling your customer offering, getting the money in on time is an existential requirement and deserves to be treated with the utmost seriousness. At all levels.

Reasons for late payment poorly understood

Partly because of this understandable bias toward creating, selling and delivering, factors that actually lead to late payment are often poorly understood.

Wherever you go in the business world and whichever sector you look at, beliefs about receivables are heavily influenced by widespread myths about why customers pay late and how (and indeed if) this can be changed at all.

Most of these are long-established, but due to technological innovation, some new ones have appeared recently.

Nine myths about late payment

It is very probable that when you try to improve receivables performance within your own company, you will have to grapple with some or all of these mistaken beliefs, in order to make real changes to how the money rolls in.

When you do your due diligence to establish the real value of adopting the Virtuous Revenue Cycle (see Part 7), or even before, when you first broach the topic of AR within your team, you will encounter some or all of the objections set out below.

Pay careful attention to these now and consider how you will respond when they arise.

They must be firmly challenged with thoughtful responses when you encounter them in your discussions with your team, as you establish your programme.

It is important to take this detour. If you are seen to be uncertain, or to lack answers, you may simply confirm or reinforce the beliefs that key individuals have wrongly held for much of their working life.

These misconceptions – and the reactions of your team when you challenge them – may also help you understand how you have been going about collecting your cash in the wrong way, which is a critical first step.

1. "We can solve receivables with (digital) tech"

We applaud technologies that help companies operate more efficiently and support growth. Automation and digitisation can reduce operating costs, accelerate cycle times, and aggregate useful data for decision-making.

But when you get paid late, it is because a human being – or human beings – have made a decision to pay you late.

A machine does what it is programmed to do. No amount of technology is going to change this, and the solution always lies in increased intimacy between people.

Significantly, in the case study in Part 3.2, even the CEO of a leading technology company admits that although technology can provide critical data to manage the business and help accelerate processes and improve communication, it *cannot get you paid quicker* because human beings make decisions on who to pay and when.

These days, nonetheless, many sellers of technology and outsourcers claim that their solutions can "solve your cash flow problems".

Sadly, some governments also support this mistaken view, perhaps because they too misunderstand the causes of late payment, but probably because digital platforms render business transactions and relationships conveniently visible to governments and regulators and aid tax collection.

If your challenge is getting paid on time, technology alone cannot solve this. It can certainly simplify some aspects of what we advocate here, but if you rely on technology alone to get your cash flow moving faster, you are heading for disappointment.

You risk investing time and money but almost certainly not becoming "first in line to get paid", unless you make the changes laid out in these chapters.

2. "We can always plug the cash gap with borrowing"

The recent tsunami of lending – enabled by years of quantitative easing – has taken the focus off AR discipline and allowed an overly complacent attitude to getting paid on time to take hold in many companies.

Fig.2.3 - THE CORONAVIRUS CRISIS HAS PUT COMPANY LIQUIDITY IN A PRECARIOUS POSITION

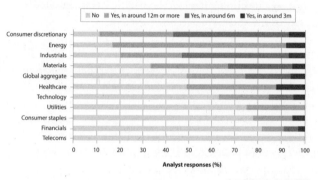

"If markets were to remain in their current state for a long time, do you expect your companies to face liquidity squeeze?"

Source: Fidelity International, April 2020

Corporate debt is at all-time highs. In some cases, governments are leaning on lenders to offer still more financial support to companies under liquidity pressure.

And make no mistake, most analysts think most companies are under a degree of liquidity pressure which will get worse (see Fig 2.3).

In several notable cases, they are making cheap funds available to lenders as well as absorbing most of the default risk to (in effect) encourage lenders to ignore the normal risk requirements which constrain their ability to lend.

Many SMEs, who do not have access to traditional bank lending, are nonetheless also being offered loans by intermediaries or secondary lenders.

There are now so many sources of funds that internet aggregators offer to take your company's details and point you to "the best deal for you" much as retail borrowers shop for mortgages online.

Many see this as a positive step that encourages competition between lenders and gives borrowers more opportunities to get help.

But all borrowing has to be paid back! Taking on debt to plug a cash gap is a risky strategy if your underlying cash flow is out of balance and if you do not at the same time take steps to bring customer payments into line.

Borrowing is an unsustainable strategy that sooner or later will come up against lending limits, increased interest rates, and risk constraints. And because it is debt, it will have to be repaid – often when you can least afford it.

Use this book to fund yourself from your own receivables – that money is yours! Avoid the unnecessary risks of increased debt. Borrow only when it clearly makes sense and will deliver operational efficiencies or growth.

3. "Getting paid conflicts with getting new business"

One of the things you will often hear, especially if you are trying to put a new focus on prompt customer payments (perhaps talking to your sales team), is: "If you press for payment (or ask us to chase the customer), you risk damaging customer relations and hindering growth."

This arresting objection, often with a specific customer cited, and sometimes phrased in the most apocalyptic terms, may very well be placed in front of you early on to deflect you.

In some cases, we have seen a sales team, as a whole, campaign against more disciplined customer payment, usually citing their deep knowledge of the market and a potentially dramatic drop in sales.

Be ready for this! Listen carefully but stick to your guns.

I have *never* seen an AR improvement programme (and I have worked in a multitude of industries all round the world for 35 years) where this supposed conflict was not brought up at some point, to challenge (or even stop dead) action to improve discipline around payment.

Be prepared for this challenge, and do not be deflected no matter how dire the predictions.

It is based on a misconception which, though widely held, is wrong. It will damage your improvement efforts if you do not challenge it.

Long experience shows that happy customers and timely invoice payment are *closely linked*. Their relationship is a symbiotic one, not an adversarial one.

In a healthy company with a Virtuous Revenue Cycle, they exist comfortably together.

Naturally, customers who have been paying you late and getting away with it will be inclined to push back when asked to change their behaviour, but provided you are aligned internally and go about your programme in the right way, you will find that they will fall into line.

And in all of these discussions we differentiate the customer who is solvent – that is, able to pay but likes to pay late – from the customer who is actually insolvent and may never be able to pay.

By adopting the VRC, we aim to identify and reduce exposure to the insolvent customer – though if possible a way forward should be sought if one can be found that does not further increase bad-debt risk – whilst mainly focusing on helping the solvent customer treat your invoices as a priority, every time.

Once you have completed your transition to the VRC and adopted what you find in this book, you will be in a stronger position in terms of available cash, healthier customer relationships and reduced exposure to bad-debt risk

4. "Customers cannot be trusted to make timely payment"

It is sometimes easier to blame the customer for slow payments than it is to tackle the real issues that cause delayed payment.

This very popular complaint absolves everyone from the need to take action – so it is very convenient for those who seek to resist change.

Yet customers are not, by and large, malign, even when they continually pay you late.

They want to hang on to their cash as long as possible. The way they do this, most of the time, is to exploit the mistakes (or omissions) that *you* make, to stretch out the time it takes them to pay.

In their own minds, they are playing the game in an ethically acceptable way whilst maximising their own free cash.

The number of customers who are really dishonest is very small. By doing your due diligence properly (see Part 2.5), you can avoid doing business with many of these in the first place.

In the vast majority of cases, if you follow our prescription and are prepared to make some basic changes to how you serve customers, you will see delayed payments reduce and eventually go away.

These changes, properly executed, will take you to a point where you have a Virtuous Revenue Cycle that uses intimacy and professional service to self-correct and deliver happy customers and timely payment.

The sequence you should follow, and Do's and Don'ts, are laid out in Part 7.

They are not all easy, but seldom do they fail, and we have seen them work in companies of all shapes and sizes, often quite quickly.

If you ignore opportunities to improve your own skills and processes, and put the blame elsewhere, such as on the customer, or the market, or on technology gaps, you will struggle to achieve lasting improvement.

In the very short term, it may feel much easier to blame others. But the real solution lies within your own organisation and requires that you be prepared to challenge and change how you think about customer service and what you do to create it.

In the service of this internal lens, you will need to incubate a culture of honesty. It needs to be okay for anyone within your organisation to call out a mistake or a need for improvement – irrespective of who may be at fault or how often it has happened.

5. "It is risky even to mention payment with many customers"

Perhaps you are under revenue pressure and badly need more sales. You cannot bring yourself to raise the topic of timely payment for *fear of giving offence* or scaring away the business.

In times of disruption, when sales are elusive, this may seem especially challenging.

The larger the customer, the more this worries you. Which is a big problem, because it is the payment habits of your big customers that you most need to change if you are to get control of AR.

I have lost count of the number of times that, when I am asked by a client for advice on how they can get paid more quickly, it quickly emerges that a clear conversation with the customer on terms and expectations has *never* been had or has not been broached for a very long time.

In reality, every customer knows perfectly well he is expected to pay. Provided you ask in the right way, at the right time, and clear away any obstacles in a supportive and efficient way, he will generally pay to terms. Clarity, civility and persistence are essential.

For new customers, we encourage you to build payment terms into your discussion from the outset – it is always easier to have these discussions at the beginning of the relationship when in the sales cycle.

You must also ensure that your agreed terms of business are written down and agreed in a credit policy.

For existing customers where you never had a written agreement, or where your agreement is very old and out of date, or where it has never come up except when invoices are already overdue, we encourage you to raise the topic as part of your new emphasis on service in order to clarify terms in writing.

On the other hand, if your late-paying customer is in fact insolvent and cannot pay you, then the sooner you know and can mitigate your risks the better.

Please note that one important reason for a reluctance to approach the customer on matters of payment may be that when payment is raised the customer has, in the past, provided a litany of shortcomings or unmet expectations which are down to repeated gaps in your own internal processes. It can be very tempting to quietly ignore these.

This is why we stress, at the heart of the VRC, the need for a disciplined mechanism for swiftly identifying unmet expectations (or discrepancies) and getting each one resolved, then preventing them from happening in the future.

Our service-based solution, described in these pages, will also bring forward your ability to spot struggling customers and to minimise your exposure to bad-debt risk.

6. "Delaying payment is always in the customer's interest"

We sometimes call this the "myth of adversarial economics" – that is, a mistaken belief that it is obviously always in the customer's own financial interest to delay payment to you and to other suppliers, while it is clearly not in yours.

In actual fact, it may be true for customers that are solvent (that is, can afford to pay) that it is often desirable to hold on to their cash longer and thus they may use any opportunity you give them to do so.

However, they usually do this by walking through doors that you leave open and need to shut!

It is also a comparatively simple exercise to demonstrate that a transaction that is prolonged and involves repeated iterations is costly not just to you, but to your customer as well. Close those gaps, the customer demonstrably saves money, and you get paid on time.

For customers who are financially healthy (i.e. are not delaying out of desperation or an actual lack of funds), the short-term benefit of hanging on to their cash longer is often offset by the transaction costs associated with delay and complexity.

It is up to you to assemble data on this, in order to demonstrate this link through empirical data and your commitment to reducing transaction costs for your customer using the VRC.

7. "Managing receivables is the responsibility of finance"

One very common problem is the low status accorded to receivables management by many companies.

Often, dealing with AR sits right at the bottom of the cultural hierarchy of importance. For example, we often find these indicators:

- The leadership team thinks receivables details are beneath them, and always delegates.
- Product designers and technical staff think their contributions are the lifeblood of the company.
- Sales and commercial teams think they are the primary creators of business, and collections are at best a distraction from important selling and at worst a big relationship and growth risk.
- Staff tasked with collections have a low status and get little support when they identify the issues preventing payment that need to be resolved by others.
- It is not uncommon for those tasked with collection to be poorly supported or even maligned when they raise issues, ask for help to resolve them or seek to unblock delayed payments.
- Frustration at a lack of support may have caused them, over time, to become reluctant even to raise issues with certain team members because of the poor response they have previously received.

These widely held attitudes have brought some of the world's most famous companies to their knees as they lead inevitably to a lack of cash.

My very first client in Asia was (at the time) the world's biggest computer company, headquartered in New York state. They recruited the cream of graduates and MBAs from all around the world. They prided themselves on their technical savvy and their ability to craft state-of-the-art solutions.

But their businesses in Thailand, Korea and China had more than a year of working capital tied up in accounts receivable. With my team, I eventually looked at their major operations in Europe and Asia, and the same challenges existed everywhere.

In their culture of top-tier excellence, invoicing and collecting monies owed was just too mundane to be of interest to the management team. Consequently their processes were clunky, full of errors and contradictions. Management interest pretty much stopped after the product had been designed and delivered.

And they came perilously close to running out of cash altogether. They neglected the basics. Their collectors were frustrated and their repeated requests for help met with disinterest or even rudeness.

The solutions that rescued them can be found on the pages of this book.

When you are too clever or too important to bother with the details of ensuring that your customer understands and agrees the terms upon which you are doing business, or creating a smooth invoice transaction, and when these attitudes become your prevailing culture, you can be sure you are not far from disaster, because customer payments will dry up.

Other obvious signs of this hierarchical challenge are common. For example, the status and pay level of employees involved in "order to cash" may well be quite low. They are far more likely to be junior and poorly paid than senior and respected, and they are unlikely to have received formal training on collections.

This status issue is, we have found, common in all geographies.

Other typical features of organisations that do not give due importance to receivables management include:
- Lack of good receivables and service data
- Absence of detailed receivables performance data from management reports and meetings
- Reluctance to discuss payment issues in leadership or sales management meetings
- A sales team that is measured and paid on orders secured or volume sold, rather than (at least in part) on cash collected.

As we will see, by consigning this critical part of the customer relationship to junior staff, companies damage not merely their cash flow but also their relationships with customers.

8. "The way to get paid quicker is to shorten payment terms"
Companies seeking earlier payment often start here. "How can we shorten our payment terms?" they ask.

Yet when we compare their stated payment terms as they already are with when they actually get paid, we find payment terms are routinely ignored by customers who consistently pay late.

The first step to getting the cash in is to get your customers to take your existing terms seriously.

Apart from anything else, if they are routinely ignoring your stated terms as they are now, why do you think that attitude will change when you shorten the terms?

Some argue, "Well, we have terms of 30 days and they pay us in 45, so if we had terms of 15 days they would pay us in 30."

This misses the fundamental point that to be first in line to get paid you need to take a binary approach to terms, whatever they are. You must expect your payment terms, once accepted and agreed, to be met.

Your VRC will remove all legitimate obstacles to timely payment and the customer will be encouraged, through service and intimacy, to pay you on time.

But he needs to have agreed the payment terms in the first place, and if he has not, shortening or offering to shorten them is unhelpful and counterproductive.

9. "It is better to play down any mistakes we make with our customers, in case they make us look bad"
Unless and until you get to grips with the things that disappoint your customers and give them opportunities to pay you late, you will never have a VRC or be first in line to get paid.

Yet some companies have cultures where executives are encouraged to report error-free relationships and over time become used to sidestepping or burying negative information.

Getting to a point where openly acknowledging errors – in order to address them – is acceptable and encouraged is an important part of the VRC and another reason why we recommend building a fact-based case for change before embarking on this programme (see Part 7).

Do
- Consider these common myths, discuss them, and find out if they are shared in your organisation and by whom.
- Add any other unhelpful beliefs which you encounter and which need to be challenged.
- Pay especial attention to functional or geographic leaders who demonstrate some or all of these mistaken beliefs. Their attitudes can wreak

havoc on your efforts to make changes and rein in AR if they remain unchallenged.

- Be aware that internal reluctance to acknowledge or grapple with invoicing or delivery issues is common because they are embarrassing, difficult or tedious to resolve.
- Note that it is also very common for a customer to be blamed for problems that really need to be solved by you and your team (we will look at why this happens and how you can handle this collaboratively later on).
- Be patient and evidence-based when you challenge unhelpful thinking in your team.

Do not

- Let worsening AR challenges convince you that customers, the market or other external parties are determined to prevent you from getting paid on time. They are not, but they may well be walking through a door that you have left open.
- Accept anecdotal evidence from anyone about what competitors, customers, etc., are doing with regard to payment. Such data are often used to excuse poor performance, or longer terms, or greater leniency, almost never to encourage better practices.
- Tolerate voices of doom who insist that attempts to regularise customer payments will alienate customers, wreck sales, be a gift to the competition, etc. – they must be challenged.
- Be persuaded that automation alone (digitisation is today's favourite solution) can solve late payment issues. Automation can be very useful but if you are being paid late it is because human beings are choosing to pay you late, and changing a traditional payment method to a digital one might reduce transaction costs but will not accelerate payment unless you take the actions we recommend here.
- Give in to the temptation to keep borrowing money to plug your working capital gap when you have significant overdue receivables. Follow this programme and collect what is owed to you. This is your money!

2.3 Forecast your cash needs

From:
When we run out of cash, we quickly find ways to plug the gap.

To:
We keep a close eye on our future cash needs so we can maintain
a healthy cash balance and have alternatives to draw on when we
anticipate a shortage.

Cash flow versus P&L

Forecasting cash flow is quite different from creating a profit and loss
account (P&L). If you read the second case study in Part 3, you will hear
about an entrepreneur who made exactly this mistake and fortunately used
the VRC to correct it.

A cash flow analysis tells you how much available cash (liquidity) you
are likely to have based upon projected growth, supplier and customer payments, and the meeting of key liabilities.

A simple way to think of it is that your cash flow forecast should match
very closely the amount of money you actually have in the bank – many
SMEs do actually think like this.

Your Profit and Loss account (P&L) might show that you are making a
healthy profit, based on an encouraging rate of growth and good margins,
whilst a close examination of your bank account might tell you that, on the
contrary, you are close to running out of cash to meet basic business needs.
Remember Margaret and her chairs?

A P&L treats an invoice as income. An invoice is not income, it is simply
a piece of paper or a digital record of the fact that you have provided a good
or a service and are owed by your customer.

Companies with healthy P&Ls go bankrupt all the time, precisely because
revenue is not income until you get paid.

The advantages of a cash forecast

If you are doing business on credit – and especially if you pay suppliers
promptly – you will discover that as you grow you need to find *more* working
capital.

This obvious dynamic nonetheless comes as a bit of a shock to many
business owners. "We are very busy," they say. "Our customers like us, we
are doing well and invoicing more every month. How can we possibly be
short of cash?"

There is nothing wrong with this dynamic as long as you have planned for it. You need to:

- Have clear credit terms
- Control credit terms so they do not lengthen unnecessarily (use BPDSO for this)
- Have a VRC and keep overdues to a minimum
- Make regular cash forecasts to reflect what is happening to growth, and to receivables

Please note that you can find tools to help you with each of these steps in this book *but* you may still find that your working capital requirement goes up and you need to plan accordingly.

Fig. 2.4 - CASH FLOW TEMPLATE

Prepared by: _____   Date: _____

Monthly Cash Flow Forecast

Select A Month To Start	July	Aug	Sept	Oct	Nov	Dec	Jan	Feb	Mar	Apr	TOTAL
Receipts											
Sales											
Other revenue											
Total receipts											
Less payments											
Direct costs											
Materials											
Stock											
Packaging											
Other											
Overheads											
Accounting											
Bank fees											
Cleaning											
Freight & postage											
Insurance											
Interest											
Marketing & advertising											
Motor vehicle expenses											
Power											
Rent											
Repairs & maintenance											
Salaries & employee expenses											
Stationery											
Subscriptions											
Telephone											
Uniforms											
Website hosting & maintenance											
Other											
Total cash payments											
Net cash flow											
Opening bank balance											
Closing bank balance											

Do

- Make a cash forecast based upon your current situation and forecast sales mix (the mix is important, because of the way it impacts BPDSO).
- In addition to your best guess, make a worst-case forecast that assumes late payment get worse and terms mix lengthens.
- Make a prudent bad-debt reserve (i.e., percentage of invoices that are outstanding but may *never* be paid).
- Prepare options ahead of time so you will be ready to deal with any developing cash gap quickly.

Do not

- Focus solely on growth and plan only to deal with cash flow issues if and when they arise.
- Ignore bad-debt risk.
- Ignore potential disruption.
- Ignore your available options for finding more working capital.
- Simply hope for the best!

2.4 Take risk seriously

From:
We are eager to sign up new customers and prefer to onboard them without delay.

To:
We routinely check new and existing customer accounts to ensure they (continue to) meet all risk criteria.

Definition of risk management
Effective risk management requires taking prudent measures when signing up new customers and when doing business with existing customers to:

- Ensure they do not present an unacceptable business risk
- Evaluate, and monitor, credit-worthiness at the outset and throughout the relationship
- Set terms
- Adjust credit and other terms as appropriate when needed
- Take other steps to protect against risk, as and when necessary
- Stop orders if and when necessary

New customers

It is simple common sense that you do not want to offer credit to a customer who presents a high risk of non-payment because of his financial situation, or of late payment because of his demonstrated prior behaviour.

Since customer circumstances may change, it is also a good idea to keep track of the changing fortunes of your customers so that, if their situation changes and they become unable to pay you, you find out as early as possible and can take action to mitigate your exposure.

This action might involve terminating business and managing the relationship to a close, or it might involve partnering with your customer to understand their predicament and agree a plan that slowly reduces your exposure but keeps them in business.

In times of disruption, the favoured option should always be to support the customer who is encountering challenges, especially if you have a history of doing business successfully with them, and if they are likely to grow again in the future.

If you can achieve the right balance of risk-mitigation and flexible support, you can strengthen an important relationship.

KYC: Know Your Customer

Companies of all sizes now have legal obligations to take steps to ensure they do not do any business with companies that are engaged in criminal activities.

Ignorance is no excuse, although if it can be shown that a disciplined process of vetting has been followed, this can mitigate penalties.

This requirement has now been adopted by 190 countries and contrary to what many believe, applies to non-regulated entities, not just regulated ones (like banks, insurance companies, etc.).

Fig. 2.5 KYC & OTHER RELATED LAWS / REGULATIONS

- US Foreign Corrupt Practices Act (FCPA)   - Monetary Authority of Singapore
- UK Bribery Act 2010   - Terrorism Suppression of Financing Act (TSOFA)

Figure 2.5 gives a snapshot of the legislation that affects companies of all sizes and sectors; other jurisdictions are adding to these all the time.

Most probably your company is a non-regulated entity, and these measures apply to you.

Because the penalties for doing business with corrupt customers are steep and rising, a level of due diligence over and above that formally required for assessing credit-worthiness is now indicated.

Here are the steps which many companies take to reduce these risks:

- Collect basic prospective customer details and record them:
  - Names and details of directors
  - Name and details of company
  - Financial and legal history
- Note that it is no longer enough to accept what the prospect says, you must take (and record) steps to verify that the prospect is who he says he is.
- By investigating your prospect using available information you can check that they are who they say they are and do not have any black marks, and using the financial data, can decide whether to offer credit and how much credit to offer.
- The yardstick for conducting sufficient customer due diligence as part of your onboarding process lies in whether, if something were to go wrong later, you would be able to satisfy a regulator that you have acted in good faith and taken reasonable steps to investigate.
- Monitor customer credit performance based upon transactions and if their credit grows beyond what has been agreed because of late payment, *stop taking new orders* until their payments are brought into line.
- In addition, regularly check their financial and credit status using reliable information and make changes to credit arrangements if necessary.
- Take steps to turn your sales force into an effective intelligence-gathering team (see Part 2.2) so you maximise your ability to detect warning signs that your customer may be having difficulty.

What does effective KYC look like?

This is not a book about KYC, but since some of what you need to do intersects nicely with what we advocate in these pages, here is a list of things you might want to consider to get ahead of the regulator!

A corporate recognition of the defined risks should be backed by policy and procedures looking at:

- Suppliers
- Customers
- Employees
  - Designers
  - Manufacturers
  - Sales

You will want to consider systems that can detect and issue early risk warnings:
- Software
- Data (internal and external)
  - Email, texts, letters, invoices, bank statements and payment records
- Reports to Management
- Supply chain log

Ensure you have defined and written down procurement best practices.

If you do already do so, have regular meetings with your bank representative and share what you are planning to do.

When you find something, promptly inform the correct people:
- Relevant authorities
- Your lawyers

There is a whole new world of risk, and governments are cash-strapped, so we can therefore expect a wave of expensive fines. By showing you are engaging in active mitigation of risks, you can impress the regulator!

Deciding whether to take on a new customer

Does it seem glaringly obvious to you that *any* new customer should be welcomed, and onboarded, with enthusiasm and gratitude?

Getting new business can be tough. Signing up a new account feels good. It may feel frustrating and even overkill to investigate your prospect's financial status.

However, it would be unwise to neglect taking this important step to guard yourself against late or non-payment, or in this new compliance-driven world, against inadvertently doing business with a customer with shady associations (see previous section).

I have seen this tricky dynamic cause a rift between finance and sales. Sales sometimes resent the chilling effect that due diligence has on the smooth acquisition of new customers.

In one company where I advised, the head of sales openly referred to the financial director as the "customer prevention officer" because the latter had inherited a high level of bad debt and overdue accounts and quite rightly wanted to instil some control in vetting new customers and setting sensible limits.

This perceived conflict is exactly that – a perceived conflict. Because there is no point in taking on a customer who cannot or will not pay, or worse still, has a shady track record.

In the former case, the consequence of inadequate risk management may be having to write off bad debts; in the latter, a swinging fine, a loss of reputation and other commercial damage may be a real possibility.

Sourcing the risk data you need

Here are the questions you need to be able to answer in the new world of KYC:

- Who are you doing business with?
- Who is doing business with them?
- What do you really know about them?
- Could they harm your business?
- What are you going to do about it?

You will probably be familiar with credit ratings agencies like Dun & Bradstreet or Thomson Reuters. There are many such services.

They can provide a credit report on your prospect and subsequent updates over time. Depending on the size of your company, they might seem expensive.

Their data, obviously, depends on publicly available information from government bodies, monetary authorities, etc.

These data, though they may be useful, are often not very current and may miss important changes in customer status which you need to know about.

They cannot foresee sudden macro shocks like epidemics or political spats – though sales intelligence can help here.

In addition, they are unable to provide the kind of KYC information you need to satisfy curious regulators that you have acted in good faith.

- Buy a report from a reputable ratings company
- Ask the customer to give you data
  - Personal details of directors
  - Credit history
  - Length of time in business
  - Customer's own DSO
  - Customer's history of bad debt
  - Customer's bank reference(s)
  - Customer's supplier reference

For KYC purposes, you may also want to secure a report from RIABU.

Deciding what terms to offer

You have options when you decide what terms to offer a customer. You can offer anything from cash in advance, to a lengthy payment term. You will want to consider:

- Are they an acceptable risk?
- What are the usual terms in your industry?
- What is the competitive situation?

1. Are they an acceptable risk?

An established company that is a household name may be worthy of credit and may appear to require a more limited level of vetting.

But household names fail every year, often leaving creditors surprised and damaged. Take nothing for granted, therefore.

2. What are the usual terms in your industry?

In setting terms, beware anecdotal evidence ("Everyone gives 90-day terms these days").

If you are an established company, you will already have a view of what terms are. (When you get paid – your actual DSO – should not be confused with theoretical trading terms!)

If you are not certain, there are independent sources you can use for benchmarking payment terms in your sector against competitors.

Remember, though, that DSOs based on company accounts – which is what ratings agencies typically use – are based on total trade receivables and therefore include the overdue portion.

Your intention should be to be conservative in the terms you grant – certainly no higher than the industry norm – and to get paid on time. You do not plan to have overdues!

3. What is the competitive situation?

Benchmarking terms against competitors is a common practice but fraught with risk.

First, are you measuring customer payment terms or actual reported DSO performance, which includes overdues and may reflect poor management or other issues?

Second, since no two companies are precisely alike in their customer mix, are you comparing like with like? The answer, almost always, is no, not exactly. Be very careful here.

Thirdly, do you want to follow what your sector is generally doing, or – given what is written in these pages – aim for a conservative but fair term? Remember this is the opportunity to communicate the seriousness with which you take payment terms, and to drive towards a shorter average DSO.

(Note that as a simple rule of thumb, if the term you offer is longer than your existing BPDSO (weighted average term), you are thereby *increasing* your weighted average and your actual DSO, even if you get paid precisely to those terms.)

Reviewing credit terms

Once you have decided that you will grant credit, you still have options:

- Very high risk – decline business, or cash in advance only
- High risk – cash in advance, or 7-day terms

- Some risk – credit terms on a trial basis, with an option to maintain or revert to cash terms
- Little risk – credit terms at or close to industry first quartile, regular review

Stop-order policy

You cannot manage risk effectively unless, having granted credit to a customer and begun doing business, you are prepared to stop or reduce business when your customer fails to meet his payment obligations.

Most companies, for this reason, have a stop-order policy based on a credit limit. The limit is typically a function of payment terms * expected business.

This means that if the actual level of business – revenue per month – substantially exceeds the forecast, the credit limit may be breached.

It can be argued that, in this case, the breach is a "good" thing as it is driven by growth. However, please note that too much growth without evidence of timely and reliable payment can be a major warning sign that something is not right.

There should therefore be a meaningful review when a limit is reached.

The fight over orders

Stopping orders can be a challenging process and may pit the salesperson against finance.

One wants the sale, and cries for an exception for his customer, for latitude, whilst the other, concerned with looming risk and bad debt, argues for discipline.

Before deciding either way, you will need to be sure that the customer is not behind on his payments because he has outstanding unresolved discrepancies.

Until you have good proactive service in place linked to discrepancy tracking and resolution, you may not actually know when the customer has an outstanding issue.

This is why when we talk about sequencing the VRC changes, we put "disciplined risk management and stop-order policy" after:

- Credit policy agreed
- Proactive contact introduced
- Discrepancies captured early
- Discrepancies resolved promptly
- Root causes analysed and tackled

Threatening to stop orders from a good-faith customer who has genuine unanswered discrepancies is to be avoided at all costs. It can be very damaging.

So you will need to be able to check potential stop-order accounts against a list of unresolved discrepancies, either manually or via an application created for that purpose.

There is simply no point in talking about risk if you are prepared to put policy aside whenever there is a chance that you might lose a sale.

Spotting customers in trouble

One of the common problems of risk management is that by the time you find out about a new risk, whether macro or micro (customer insolvency, border dispute, pestilence), it is often too late to do anything about it.

Major credit agencies typically report such things after they have already happened and have a distinctly patchy track record of anticipating insolvency.

Note that trade credit insurers with their ability to gather intelligence from multiple sources can help here – see Part 5.2.

It therefore makes sense to think creatively about other ways to spot customer risk ahead of time, so as to avoid depending on agencies and other external sources.

These can include:

- A change in customer payment patterns (proactive contact really helps here, by giving you early insight into changes in customer behaviour):
  - Delayed payments without clear justification
  - Unavailable or unresponsive staff
  - An increase in reported discrepancies, of a kind which seem questionable or arbitrary (a sudden spate of lost paperwork, absent signatories, or plain old silence) can be red lights – but note that unless you are in early contact and paying attention you will not be able to spot them
- Commercial intelligence gathered by your team from:
  - Customer visits and discussions
    - E.g. An increase in visible stock on a customer site may suggest a slowing of business – ask to walk around the warehouse and despatch area
    - A friendly chat with customer staff, including your buyer, may reveal anxiety about headcount reductions, loss of an important customer
  - Competitor interactions (seasoned salesmen generally know their competitor counterparts, and these should be cultivated)
  - Industry forums and professional bodies where the chitchat includes varying customer fortunes
  - Trade credit insurers (see Part 5)

This is sufficiently important to justify special sales training – so that customer interactions and conferences and other forums are approached in a disciplined way – and we address the "intelligence-gathering" aspect of sales training in Part 4.

Do
- Always carry out a proper credit check of a new account, including any informal market intelligence.
- Ensure that you include the new KYC requirements – penalties are dire.
- Be prepared not to do business when red flags go up, or at least to investigate further.
- Collect intelligence from third parties, including credit rating agencies and the customer's own bank(s).
- Collect intelligence from your own network and your own sales team.
- Push back with clear reasons if you come under pressure to proceed in the face of significant negative intelligence.
- Be ready to limit credit or insist on cash terms if payment history gives concern. You can start cautiously and extend credit based upon performance.
- For existing accounts, do regular credit checks, and where payments slow or other factors warrant it, conduct ad-hoc checks via agencies and via your team.

Do not
- Be intimidated into taking on unacceptable customer risk – the stakes are now higher than they have ever been.
- Grant credit where you see reasons to be cautious – you can always limit credit and extend terms subject to performance.
- Fail to monitor customer payments and increase monitoring when they slow.
- Neglect to conduct periodic checks, especially on large customers.

2.5 Insolvent customers and bad debt

This book is concerned with describing what an effective receivables management process looks like, and how to build one with a minimum of delay or confusion.

At the heart of what we have called the Virtuous Revenue Cycle is the notion of early and constant customer contact.

Once adopted, this model should accelerate payments from solvent customers of good will and give you an enhanced ability to spot problems early when a customer – for whatever reason – is struggling to meet his payment obligations.

But even the best company, from time to time, will find itself with a customer who has not responded to attempts to improve intimacy and remove obstacles to delayed payment.

In times of disruption, such customers may become more common, so it will be important to have internal agreement in how to deal with them.

When a debt becomes chronic, you must first take steps to understand what you are dealing with:

- Are you constantly failing to meet expectations? (Always start with an honest internal look)
- If not, why is the customer not paying you?
  - He has genuine cash flow issues and is struggling.
  - He is managing his cash aggressively and does not care about his behaviour.
- How important is this customer to you, and how much is at stake?

Not meeting expectations

When you have a disagreement with a customer and he is paying you late, start by assuming that it is rooted in a misunderstanding.

Proceed on the basis that you are open to feedback and keen to improve. Send in a senior person, if necessary, to unblock the situation (especially if tempers are frayed).

In our second case study, the CEO of a start-up discovered that when he took the trouble to lunch a customer's staff he was able to unblock payment. Absence of attention had allowed things to deteriorate.

Sometimes you may be surprised to discover that the same error on your part – of action or omission – has been occurring for quite a while and that delaying payment is the customer's way of getting your attention.

If this is true, then the failure is yours, not his. Ask him to explain, again, what has gone wrong, with specific examples.

Genuine cash flow issues

If he is genuinely short of cash to pay you, then you must quickly establish: Is this temporary and is his business basically sound? Or is this a sign of impending insolvency or worse?

There are a number of ways to check his status, and you should act without delay.

Before you go see him and ask, you should encourage your salesman to learn what he can from visits, observation, and competitor and market feedback.

You should also conduct an immediate credit check (see Part 9 for agencies you can use for this).

Temporary cash flow issues

A good customer may occasionally be short of cash. If all real impediments to payment have been sorted out but your customer still cannot pay you what he owes you in full, you should consider cutting a deal. Remember:

- You want him to stay in business
- You have a future together
- You do not want to fall out

First, you are committed to a long-term relationship. Second, you are prepared to strike a deal for continuing supply provided the net amount owed to you reduces every month.

This means that each month the value of cash paid must exceed that of new invoices issued. This is a widely recognised approach and is sometimes called the "reducing balance" approach.

In this way he stays in business, and your debt comes down. You will need to decide how long he should be allowed to regularise his account, but consider 6–12 months as a guide.

Impending insolvency

As soon as you learn that a customer is likely to go out of business, act to minimise your losses. Before you notify him of stopped supply, give him a chance to make an offer of payment on the "reducing balance" principle. The first payment will need to be agreed and paid promptly, or the deal is off. If appropriate (but it may be too late), introduce him to a potential lender.

If all attempts at a deal fail or if promises are made and not met – he may well be desperate – then move quickly to stop supply and collect what's due to you.

Note: This book is not about pursuing bad debts but about avoiding them. Look elsewhere for lots of excellent advice on how to pursue a failing or failed customer.

Part 3
Case studies

3.1 Background

If you have receivables challenges, or if you are launching a new business and want to avoid them, there is nothing like learning from the mistakes of others.

We have chosen three case studies featuring experienced leaders from very different businesses explaining, in their own words, how they adopted the principles in this book, in each case relatively early in their tenure.

They were able not merely to master the art of getting paid on time – in one case avoiding an impending cash crisis – but to use the power of the Virtuous Revenue Cycle and its positive impact on customer intimacy to identify other critical business issues and find growth and structure.

If you are fortunate enough to be a start-up, you may want to read this section in conjunction with Part 6, so you can indeed start off on the right foot!

These leaders' efforts to put getting paid on time centre-stage were not easy, nor always welcomed with enthusiasm by board or employees. But their enthusiasm for these solutions and their spectacular financial and personal achievements speak for themselves.

We have deliberately included this section early in the book to encourage you to see the benefits of this approach and to persevere when obstacles arise, as they certainly will.

The first study features a technology company whose revenue grew from US$400m in 2004 to more than US$5bn in 2020. Their CEO explains how following the principles laid out here – he was an early adopter of the Virtuous Revenue Cycle – helped create a firm foundation for healthy growth and positive cash flow.

For Bill Padfield, getting the "customer to cash" cycle right at Datacraft was about a lot more than just getting paid – it was an essential part of a healthy business and involved the CEO, sales leaders, and the whole team adopting a binary approach to customer engagement and service.

The second case takes us into the mind of engineer-turned-entrepreneur Mike Grundy, who established a specialty chemicals company but ran into early cash flow issues due to rapid growth and lack of awareness of the cash flow implications of this apparently positive dynamic.

By adopting a binary approach to payment terms, taking a direct and active interest in customer intimacy (including personally travelling to key markets and meeting key admin and payments staff), he overcame a potentially disastrous early cash shortage and built a war chest for growth.

The third example takes us into the oil services business at a time when collapsing crude prices were squeezing margins and cash flow. Despite a lack of scale, despite being a start-up, Peter Hone used relationships and trust to ensure that his company was first in line to get paid. In his words, "Trust gets paid."

3.2 The MNC: Cash is reality

In 1997, Bill Padfield moved to Singapore to do a turnaround on a newly listed business called Datacraft, at the time Cisco Systems' largest partner in Asia-Pacific.

In 2020 he retired as Chairman of NTT, a $4.5bn tech services company that had absorbed Datacraft and its parent, Dimension Data.

Back in 1997, Datacraft, operating in 14 markets in Asia, had innumerable problems, were under investigation by the SSE, and were also running into receivables challenges.

Bill found a growth culture, driven by the internet boom, where everything was about sales, no one talked about receivables, and China DSO was 1,000 days.

When told "This is normal in China", Bill replied, "1,000 days of receivables is not normal for anywhere on this planet. Maybe some other planet!"

He set to work to change the culture entirely.

Cash is reality
From day one we adopted the basic premise that revenue is only vanity, profit is sanity, but cash is reality.

We needed a new leadership culture used to driving the business by a balanced set of metrics, and no longer being a "hero culture", where it's all about just bringing home a sale.

Metrics

We refocused on a limited range of metrics, including obviously our balance sheet. There needed to be balance. It is great to do what you want and grow like crazy if you have benevolent investors, but are we trying to generate cash as much as we can? Make sure you track those metrics.

I got the company really focused on building a strategy map, and moved the whole company over to balanced scorecard.

Management

We had to make sure that we had the management who understood how to manage a business using (balanced scorecard) metrics rather than "I've got a friend I play golf with who can give us a deal".

We needed to formalise the working capital part of our performance.

In the early days it was all about bringing the leadership team up to that level that understood this balanced business model and why we needed those metrics in place.

The Three Ss

Simplicity

A business with many customers and many solutions in many – often very different – markets is a complicated mechanism.

So we focused on creating simplicity with a few clearly defined themes in just the right balance. We reinforced this culture by using acronyms – because you can stick them on the wall, on coasters, on T-shirts.

I guess the keyword was focus. If you haven't got these things clear in your mind, you can be challenged!

If you brought in any member of my management team here right now and asked, "What are the key metrics?" – they could all recite them off by heart.

Sales

We really focused on sales to make sure we had the right sales model to go to market and that we could migrate from selling products on a transactional basis to building more annuity contracts.

This required a focus on specific customers and solutions, and on building a specific set of sales skills which would now include ownership of profit outcomes – from contract to cash.

In other words, a customer relationship needed to deliver a defined contribution in revenue and margin terms, and what it delivered needed to match what was built into the deal at the front without leakage. And this included working capital leakage.

Solutions

The last one was: "What solutions are we taking to what markets?" You cannot be a master of everything, so we focused on cutting down the number of different solutions we offered and on cutting the number of clients we worked with, so that we could focus, focus, focus.

Speed and pressure

We had to report every 90 days so we needed to move fast. I knew that if we didn't show rapid change I might not last long.

We needed to be in disaster mode. We could not afford to be in "business as usual" mode, and in creating that pace and urgency we found we were all running 100-hour weeks regularly.

Once you hit the tipping point, magic starts to happen

From a CEO perspective, it all comes down to personal focus, never mind the business focus. When the results started to improve, you could see the change in sentiment within the board, the change in sentiment with employees and, more importantly, the change in sentiment with the shareholders.

Receivables and the VRC

Now we still had this problem with receivables because we needed the cash. Anything you want to do in a successful and rapidly growing business requires cash. Full stop.

This is when I ran into Mr Littlewood. To be honest, when we met and Simon talked about his Virtuous Revenue Cycle, my first reaction was "Yes, sure..."

Then during subsequent conversations it became very clear that he knew what he was talking about. And as I learned more about the business, his ideas fitted our challenges.

With Simon and his team we engaged in a period of value discovery over a few months and we defined and structured the quote-to-cash process using Simon's VRC concept.

To begin with, just generating a quote was costing us thousands of dollars. Plus we were generating quotes like crazy for anything.

This is again Simon's area of expertise. That meant that suddenly as we made the changes we were generating cash.

We started from a 120-day DSO – with 1,000 days in China! – and eventually, believe it or not, we got to an 18-day DSO.

Problems of success

But suddenly we were faced with success problems! Do we do a buyback of shares on the open market or do we make further investments?

In the end we were generating cash at such a successful level that we were able to do shareholder walk-throughs to very satisfied audiences.

Sales culture

As Simon always says, a lot of the problems with getting paid on time are actually embedded in the behaviour of the sales team because they are the ones talking to the customer.

They are the ones who might possibly circumvent some of the things that your finance department is putting into place, like a credit policy.

A salesman may say to the customer, "No worries. Just give me the order. You can pay whenever you feel you can manage."

This was a big change in the culture of the salesperson. The principle of hit-and-run just had to go. This whole idea of landing a deal and disappearing – that was no longer going to cut it!

There was already a very good principle in place in the company, which was that the sales guy didn't get paid until we'd been paid, but we just enforced it more, and that changed behaviour significantly.

I was not terribly popular in driving this home, as you can imagine.

Previously when a guy came in with a purchase order, he thought that the party should start. "Thank you very much. Well done!"

But cash is reality. So now it's when the money comes in that we have a big party!

I can remember the days of being the sales guy myself and it's not just the money, it's the recognition. You want to be seen as successful by your peers, so you reinforce the cultural change by doing the recognition of the success at the right time.

Customer onboarding and quotation process

We had to make sure that during the prospecting and in the pipeline review we were actually setting deals up to be successful.

Before we closed a deal, we needed to make sure that we properly understood the structure of the deal, especially the key milestones – because these are complex IT projects mixing hardware and consultancy.

You have to make sure the terms are crystal-clear. That starts with the very first engagement of the salespeople within the consulting team. It can't be after the fact.

Many companies still face exactly the same issues, and if they don't address them in the early stages those issues can come back to bite them in a very, very big way.

Policy and tone from the top

The data you collect at the outset basically sets the tone for whether your customer thinks that you take payments and pricing seriously or whether it's just an afterthought.

You really do have to set the right tone on this. The chairman of our business at the time came in from the banking world, an expert on mergers, acquisitions and so on. He sat in on board meetings.

He would say, "I don't want to see the receivables policy or the receivables summary – I want to see everything! Even the $10k that is 180 days old. I want to see that $5k. Why hasn't that been settled?"

What I learned from this and still carry with me is I examine every receivable, not just the big ones.

Constant focus

Believe me, this will become part of your culture, but it's got to be done consistently, driven from the top, and kept up.

The moment you think it's taken care of and you move on to something else, it goes back exactly the way it used to be, unless it's all done through automation – and very few companies have got to that point yet.

Force down the ownership

As CEO – just one man – you just do not have the time to do it yourself, so you have got to force this stuff down into a leadership team that you truly trust and hold those people accountable.

Ultimately, my CFO would be tracking this data, reporting into me, and I would be taking my time on the exceptions.

If you're doing it yourself 100% of the time, then clearly you will not have time for anything else.

As a CEO, most of your meetings should be 15, 20 minutes long. In my view, if you go beyond that and you're sitting in a meeting for two hours, you are wasting your time – you should be there judging and deciding and stepping in on exceptions.

Revenue recognition

In your contract with the customer in a complex business where there is a combination of products and services being delivered and you are keen to win the business – if in the enthusiasm of the sale you kind of let those things that should be clearly stated remain ambiguous, then you're setting yourself up for a situation where you bill and the customer doesn't recognise it.

A clearly defined quotation leads to clearly defined and collectable billing. So we made sure the salesperson had the right support from a commercial expert (we had a lot of good accountants inside the company, but they were not necessarily the right people to construct commercial contracts).

We also had lawyers inside the company and needed to accept this crossover point between sales, legal and financial. We hired some really good commercial heads who understood how to structure these deals in the first place and were also the kind of people that could sit next to the salespeople and sales team in front of the client, negotiating or leading the negotiations. That became a big difference.

First the salespeople needed to trust them – and initially their nick-name was "the sales prevention team" because these guys "are always trying to stop my deals".

If you're not going away happy saying we want to do more business at this level, something is wrong on one or both sides of the equation, so the commercial team added a huge amount of value and that has become quite a substantial structure inside the organisation on a global basis.

SMEs today

If you are an SME, and you're struggling to get your much bigger customers to pay you because they're rather good at holding onto their money, you can borrow money – but is that really a good solution?

Message for start-ups

I am spending a significant amount of my time with tech start-ups, looking at them from both a funding point of view and also what I call a "parental supervision" point of view.

These start-ups are looking for experience of how to grow, how to enter new markets, how to develop the business – which is something I like doing.

But with incredibly low interest rates on borrowing, it can lead them into very bad discipline.

How long interest rates will be low I do not know, but whatever the answer, you can't have that kind of behaviour for long – it is not sustainable.

Indeed if we look at what's happened with SMEs and DSOs over the last few years, not just in Singapore but globally, there is an overwhelming trend for small to medium-sized enterprises to get paid later and later and later on for the larger companies to manage their cash flow more effectively.

This trend is very evident and to some extent I think has been somewhat encouraged by the credit flushing about.

Be ready to say no

At some point, you've got to have the discipline inside your company to say "I'm sorry but no" to a customer who wants longer terms or who simply won't pay on time.

This is awkward, especially when dealing with a very large customer. It is therefore critical you set it up right in the beginning.

Fortunately, though, the tech companies that I'm working with at the moment are nearly all starting businesses in the annuity services world, so it's very easy to stop the services if you want to ensure payment.

In the old world it was purely transactional – you transact something, you transfer title to the client, and it would be the end of it, and then you sit there waiting indefinitely to get paid.

Discrepancies and safety culture

People are often far too keen to blame the customer for non-payment. But quite often it is an internal failure – not a customer failure – as expectations had been set and often not documented in the sales process.

In the early days there were things that were agreed outside of the contract. There were handshakes done on golf courses.

Things like "I know we said next August but will get it done by July" can come back to bite you when they are not written down.

So we started a bid review board for big jobs to make sure we had the thing structured properly before we even started work.

Culture of honesty

One of the things we commonly fight – perhaps slightly more in Asia – is the reluctance to acknowledge where these off-piste conversations occurred and where things were done that damage your margin outcomes.

The challenge is to create a culture of honesty where people actually face up to the discussions that were held.

You want it so that the guys can say, "We didn't get it right. We thought this was this and it ended up as that."

For this to happen, team members must feel safe to talk about it. The moment you have a case of "If I find you got this wrong, I will come down on you hard", that's a culture of fear. Then people keep quiet and you learn nothing. So you have to have a culture of safety, too.

Reliability is a big plus

One of the things we were very proud of is our reliability. Suppliers used to call us a metronome or a Swiss watch and they knew that we would always pay on the day.

Once we built up a history then, well, if the date just moved a bit, they had confidence and trust and we were fine.

Human contact and trust, *not* technology

It is not really a technology question to get paid on time. It is more about human trust. You have to build your trust all the way through your supply chain. The more you can do that, the better.

3.3 The SME: See it as love

Mike Grundy is a self-made entrepreneur who started a specialty chemicals company from scratch, then achieved revenues in the order of US$100m before selling half of it to a private equity fund in 2016.

Early on in his journey, he worked with the author to address a major cash flow challenge which threatened the very survival of the business.

Mike explains how the experience of entrepreneurship taught him about the realities of having balance sheet discipline all through the business, starting with leadership from the top.

Background

I worked in paper mills in England and later I worked for an American chemical company supplying to those paper mills which in 1996 took me out to Singapore.

I was running the region over here. And I really loved it, it was great.

Then in 1998, the company I worked for was acquired by another American company and everything changed.

They had overpaid for the acquisition and that created enormous pressures. It was a very, very unpleasant cultural shift. The work ethic changed. There was huge pressure on short-term results, and we hated it.

In 2000 my colleague and I decided to leave and have a go on our own.

Amazon Papyrus

Why did we choose the name Amazon Papyrus? Papyrus is the Egyptian word for paper, so that's pretty obvious.

We chose Amazon because we had absolutely nothing! We had no money, no customers, and we wanted to make ourselves sound big. The Amazon Forest is massive. The Amazon River is massive.

In short, we felt that adopting that name made it sound like we were a much bigger company than we really were.

We were so successful in this effort to appear bigger that when we showed a potential customer in Thailand a picture of a production plant in America – which was actually from a supplier of ours – our prospect said, "Guys, you're much bigger than the companies we normally deal with!"

What is our business?

As a specialty chemicals company, we are selling chemicals and service. We are a problem-solving company, and our people are actually stationed at our customers' paper mills.

We understand the customers' systems and processes very well, so that we can then help solve problems in production. When by applying chemical technology – new molecules – we can improve their efficiency by 2% or 3%, that's worth a lot of money to them, because paper plants are huge and costly. Big pulp and paper mills cost US$300m–$400m to build and run 24/7.

For our customers, getting the most efficiency out of these huge investments is vital and we bring our expertise to the table along with the chemicals to help solve their problems.

We provide chemicals and we control their use so that they have measurable impacts on our customers' output and economics. And we constantly evaluate, fine-tune and innovate. We keep track of new technology – new and innovative molecules – so that we can constantly bring more value to our customers and sell them more product.

The journey

We just had our 20-year anniversary. Because of COVID, it was a huge Zoom meeting with 450 people in all regions.

But if we go back to those early days it was very tough. We did not really have an office. We were using an old printing works as a little bit of space and a printing works in the far end of Hong Kong.

The first business plan – entirely right, entirely wrong

We built a business plan showing the first three years, and that proved to be very accurate in terms of revenue numbers, wrong in terms of customer.

In terms of numbers, what we thought would happen did happen, and we never moved more than 5% away from our business plan, as far as revenue was concerned.

That sounds like brilliant planning – but actually it wasn't!

What we had thought would happen is that the customers we already knew well would come over with us, because they trusted us, because we already had a relationship.

In reality that did not happen. Because they knew us so well (and whence we had come), they really put us through the wringer. We had to go through every single step of the sales process with no shortcuts.

On the other hand, some new customers we didn't know at all were more open to saying, "Well, here are some young upstarts, let's give them a chance."

So in fact it was the reverse of what we expected. But we came out with pretty much the same revenue numbers as our forecast – just not in the way we had put in our plan!

We missed two things in that plan.

First, we underestimated the expenses. Revenue and margin held up well, but we were way over on expenses. Secondly, and worse, we very quickly got into cash problems.

There were many times where my partner and I just could not get paid. We had to wait until our customers paid us, before we could get a salary.

We asked ourselves: "We are growing nicely. The P&L shows that we are making money. But where's the cash?"

How salesmen think

We were – are – a bunch of salesmen, so when we got short of cash we naturally tried to solve the problem by selling more.

And the more we sold, the faster we grew, the more desperate we got for cash. I liked to think that I understood cash flow before I started Amazon Papyrus. Clearly I didn't!

At three years we were doing fine revenue-wise but the cash problems were constant.

Fortunately I met Simon of RIABU and asked for his help to understand "Where is the cash?"

In those days I did not even fully understand working capital – we were all salesmen! Simon came in, did some work for us, explained our gaps, and told us about the Virtuous Revenue Cycle.

This work opened our eyes to start really thinking about what we were doing with receivables (and also inventories).

We had not watched receivables closely enough. We were dealing in countries like India and China, where the tradition is to hold the money until the supplier absolutely screams.

Growth is great

Growth is great, but if you don't understand the relationship between working capital and sales growth, you might find you need more working capital, not less.

When you grow fast, this lack of insight is a very common issue. And the reason most start-ups go bust (I now understand) is not a lack of customers – it's lack of cash!

Holding the red line on payment terms

No company, especially a start-up, can afford to take a relaxed or flexible view on payment terms.

Simon said something that has stuck with me to this day which I have repeated many, many times to the team as it has grown.

You go to a customer and you negotiate your price and you also negotiate your payment terms.

Imagine that when it comes to the time for payment the customer says, "Well, on reflection I am not going to pay the price we agreed. I am going to pay you 5% less." You would argue strongly that they should honour the price that was agreed on.

But mostly you don't defend payment terms in the same way – which if you think about it is illogical and plain wrong.

If they agreed 30-day payment terms but then unilaterally decided to pay you in 60, you should not accept this any more than you would accept an arbitrary drop in price.

Both of these are red lines that you should hold. Going back something like 17 years, this has stayed with me and is something I repeat to my sales team even today to try and get that discipline in.

Owning it from the top

I think that my direct involvement – visible ownership from the head of the company of what was and was not being paid – was a way of showing the importance of this aspect of the customer relationship.

It is always counter-productive to get aggressive with customers. I would not recommend banging the table under any circumstances.

What I did first was to personally go and see the customers to establish who was actually making payment decisions – normally the accounts department, as it turned out.

Over time I got to know the accounts departments of our customers and took them out for lunch. A finance lady in the Philippines said, "I've never been taken out to lunch before."

After that I could phone her up and she would always answer. And over time, by investing in relationships whenever and wherever I travelled, I collected the phone numbers of people I could call and ask for payment.

I also went further with another customer where they were not paying. I had been calling the office without a result. I asked for – and got – the owner's mobile phone number and I called him directly and badgered him. He was a bit surprised. But he paid!

Lead by example

We started at the top and then I went to see the people within the customer who actually were in charge of releasing our money – then we taught all our sales force how to do the same.

I switched from being a salesman always focused on trying to get new business, which is essentially where I started my career, and my new priority became to get cash in. Without that crucial change, the company could have died!

Getting salespeople to see this bigger picture was the next step.

Frankly, in those very early days we lacked education and were almost like a child growing up. So we set about educating our team on the balance sheet. We made receivables a core part of sales training and performance measurement.

More recently, we have graduated to systems and processes and become more professional. Now we have a CFO who has been very focused on this.

For example, the sales team get reports on any late payments. They know exactly where they are at any time and have to follow up.

With customers who are behind, we follow the "reducing balance" policy. We say, "Look, in order for us to go on supplying you, give us $100 and we will deliver $70 worth of products, so that our receivables exposure visibly reduces."

We know that if we can help customers overcome a payment problem, we retain the business and strengthen the relationship.

Back in 2008, many of our customers were in financial trouble and if we had just set firm limits and stopped supply we would have lost their business. Instead, we worked together with them and in most cases we have come out the other side with a strong relationship.

Remember it is often not that someone is deliberately trying to avoid paying on time, but that they have a genuine problem themselves.

It is key to understand the customer's situation. We are going through a similar period of disruption right now with COVID.

Do whatever you are able to do to help customers who genuinely want to work with you but have issues.

Managing risk carefully and mobilising sales
In the current crisis, we became concerned about customers running into cash flow problems, so we monitored that much, much more closely than we would normally.

There have been some issues but because we paid close attention we were able to spot them and control them early.

Role of sales
Customer intelligence is key. You monitor what their cash flow position is – some are publicly quoted companies, so you can track their data.

As a service-intensive company, we can have 10–15 people on a customer's site. We can get a first-hand feel for the customer, and of course we have learned to talk to our competitors and other suppliers and to get a feel from them for what the situation is on site.

Informed view of salesmen

Our salesmen at the end of the day understand our customers' model and processes in detail. They have usually spent long periods on site so they know all the customer's people, technical and administrative.

With practice they have become a valuable part of our intelligence-gathering mechanism. We want to understand as early as possible where a customer is struggling so we can reach out.

On a big, big industrial site where there are many people, they meet the people and can see the level of activity and product and materials going in and out.

Experienced salesmen can spot potential trouble and gently chase up payments, and they can find out from competitors whether they are also experiencing payment delays or other issues.

Sales education is key

This is one key part of our intelligence-gathering process and we also do a course to lay out principles and share learnings.

Education is key. You really cannot just put in a new written credit and receivables policy for your team to read and expect things to change.

Often a few painful lessons are needed, like when a salesman suddenly discovers his bonus is less than he expected because some of his customers paid late.

"You should have understood it" is our message. "Now do you understand it?"

His dismay is understandable (especially if he has been earning good bonuses based solely on revenue) and it is therefore very instructive.

We have not lost any employees because of this – because we have continued to invest in communication and education.

We sat down with the teams and gave them some basic financial education and training and explained the fundamental facts about the business impacts of late payment.

This sounds very basic but I like to do a drawing of a bucket with holes in it, and a tap with water coming into the bucket. This represents our business. If we have too many holes, we have no profit in it and we risk running out of cash.

Getting the sales team on board

Do the education, wait for a few painful lessons, and slowly the team will get on board. They may also need to understand this change in the context of their personal finances.

"How would you feel if I don't pay you at the end of the month? Or if this month I pay you two weeks late?"

Simon encouraged us to talk about something called the Virtuous Revenue Cycle, which starts usually with firmly setting clear expectations.

When commencing a relationship with a new customer, talk about the importance of both price and terms and make it clear from the very start that terms and price are both not optional.

Written credit terms

To ensure that this is clear, you should have a formal policy written down for every proposal. The terms are discussed and agreed upfront and all documentation reinforces the message.

Otherwise, if the customer senses that you are not serious, and that these things are not important to you, they will pay someone else first and wait until you ask.

I remember years ago I received an analysis from accounts that a customer had not paid us for nearly a year. I went and saw the customer and he said with a smile, "Well, you come from a very rich American company. You don't seem to be bothered."

We had not made it clear that we took timely payment seriously, and so our customer waited for us to ask.

Customers will always pay the suppliers that are the most persistent.

See it as love rather than being a nuisance. Do whatever it takes. Your invoice needs to be always at the top of the pile rather than disappear to the bottom.

Is being paid a distraction?

For some people, taking these additional steps may seem like a bit of a distraction. After all, they are in the business of making stuff, delivering services. This idea that "Yikes, now I have to take the finance lady out for lunch" may seem like something that's non-core.

But a commercial company like Amazon Papyrus is about one thing, which is making money. If you are just making and delivering products and not getting paid, you are wasting your time.

So you've got to keep cash flow absolutely in the front of your mind and stick to this message in a disciplined way. If you have this discipline within your company and your sales team, the customer soon gets to know who you are and knows that you will be knocking on the door.

Digital communication

In the new COVID world where the salespeople cannot travel, there are new digital possibilities.

This whole disruption has opened our eyes to the different tools that are out there. We are using Zoom for training and management meetings and things like that.

As far as customer meetings are concerned, it will be interesting how this develops for us. We now have 330 salespeople out there. Our travel costs – international and even local – are high, and now even customers (who are in the same boat, after all) may actually be willing to adopt Zoom meetings.

But we will always need to have some face-to-face. Sometimes you need to have a beer with people to build that relationship. But if face-to-face is interspersed with Zoom meetings and that keeps a relationship going and saves us money, that will be a thing that's important for us.

Technology does not get you paid faster

People buy from people, and people pay people. That's why we always talk about people in the context of getting paid on time, rather than looking for a technology solution to fix it.

There are start-ups in Singapore and elsewhere being created all the time, and one of the things that we try to tell start-ups is "Don't neglect this side of things!"

Yet even now with record insolvencies among SMEs, if you look at the incubators that banks, say, have launched to help start-ups, there is never anything about cash flow.

Everything is about communication, product development and borrowing money.

I have joined an angel investing club arm and do some investments in and mentoring start-ups.

What is clear is some of these guys have got fantastic ideas, fantastic insights on technology and different things, yet they have no idea about the business side, no idea about managing cash, no idea about marketing.

And that's what's missing. So it doesn't surprise me that so many, sadly, fail.

3.4 The start-up: Trust gets paid

Peter Hone, a 30-year oil and gas industry veteran whose background includes a spell with Lloyds, helped launch ModuResources, an oil services company.

ModuResources, which provides a range of rig services to owners and operators throughout the well life-cycle, began life in a period of low oil prices and great stress.

Peter found that amidst a general shortage of cash, it was close relationships that kept the money coming in. With good relationships across the industry, ModuResources was able to grow rapidly, and within three years of start-up, they had 50 staff and had won contracts with some of the oil majors.

ModuResources

The oil services industry is notorious for late payment. 90-day terms turn into 120 turn into 180.

Our customers are short of cash and will always take an opportunity to delay payment. Unless we make a point of getting close to them, demonstrating that we feel their pain and helping them find solutions, we are just like any other supplier looking to get paid. And we will fail!

Pressure to cut costs has caused the industry to shed many older more experienced staff – losing both expertise and relationships. It's common to hear the term "in-country value" which is shorthand for (sacking expensive expatriates and) localising the team. Great for reducing operating costs, not so good for either technical depth or relationships.

Find their pain

With less experienced teams in-country we have found it critical to educate the team on the need to visit customers, get to know them, and understand their processes and pain points.

Operators – especially the larger ones – often have multiple finance teams and each one is responsible for supporting a particular asset.

Unless you take the trouble to find out who they are, visit them, and build a relationship, you will be at a real disadvantage and will not be first in line to get paid.

Abundant cash led to inefficiency

In the past, the industry was awash in cash, and as a consequence rates were high. It was not hard to get paid on time, but this abundance led to generally relaxed and inefficient processes. Duplication, errors and a lack of discipline were common.

For a supplier like us, prepared to get into the details, this new pressure to find efficiencies, eliminate waste and do more with less represents an opportunity.

Go the extra mile by listening to the client and finding solutions and anything is possible – including getting paid promptly even in an environment where many suppliers (who have not understood the changed environment) are being paid later and later.

Smarter than the competition
If you have a relationship, its harder for them to ignore you!

Because of the stress on getting growth at the beginning, we had ignored cash and collections. The faster we grew, the more cash we needed to put in – till we understood the dynamic, we were unable to influence this.

We were only 3 months old when Simon came in and helped us. Based on his advice, we went to a client's offices in KL. We learned heaps about how they operated – multiple entities and complexities – and as a result we got everything paid in two weeks and learned a valuable lesson.

Simon said (and to be honest, as a bunch of engineers this wasn't what we wanted to hear): "Waiting till the end of the transaction and then arguing over the invoice is an outdated way to behave, and because it's what most other companies do, it won't help you get paid."

Though I knew about DSO from my MBA, it was not a concept that really lived for us.

Simon helped us model DSOs and understand how DSO can be influenced – by owning cash outcomes right from the beginning.

DSOs are now down to 80 – from more than 200. This is the result of focusing on the right things from the very beginning of each relationship.

It's simple but it's hard
You get caught up in the details. We are engineers, but we needed to embrace the need for intimacy – right from the start.

Once we actually did that, and made that difficult cultural change, we found that the cash started to roll in and DSO came down.

Now we are in a sector where over the past two years average DSOs have grown steadily – but ours has halved!

If you can make them need you – and you do this by listening and acting over and over again – then they will want to do business with you.

If you show you care, you will keep your customer. If you do not, then someone else will, and your customer will be gone. I suspect this is true cross-industry.

Cycle of communication

Of course things go wrong when you are delivering complex services under time pressure. In the old days, we would find out where a customer was unhappy only after we had asked and failed to get paid.

So as well as understanding how the customer operates from the very outset we need to ensure our consultant – who's there on the spot doing the work – properly understands the client's needs and keeps up active communication so we can learn early about any possible friction points.

Because consultants are mostly third-party contractors, we have learned that we need to invest time in making sure that they are comfortable and are schooled in how to stay close to the client who is probably a rig supervisor or another engineer.

This was difficult to begin with and remains difficult now.

Getting started was hard

We started ModuResources confident in our expertise. But the industry has changed, and we are all engineers, not experts in managing cash and certainly not experts in relationships.

I was fortunate that our chairman had the foresight to let me bring in Simon early on so that we could understand the dynamics of a Virtuous Revenue Cycle (which was a very strange concept to us) and then, starting with some conceptual illustrations, begin to "walk the talk" and build service and intimacy into all our discussions from front to back.

From the chairman to the leadership, to the sales team, to the consulting team, to the back office – everyone has gradually become tuned to the need to look for opportunities to improve service.

This small investment at the beginning changed our approach, alerted us to the need for a company-wide focus on service and intimacy, and led to a big reward.

3.5 Key lessons

These cases usefully demonstrate the key principles of the Virtuous Revenue Cycle, albeit in different ways and at different points in each company's own business cycle.

Whether you call it "mindfulness" or "intimacy" or plain old "customer service", each one of these highly successful executives unhesitatingly cites active engagement with customers from the very beginning of the relationship as the key "getting paid on time" differentiator.

Note that they also warn against treating automation – however compelling – as a substitute for human intimacy.

Let us summarise the key learnings from these three success stories, placed in the context of this book and its focus on service and engagement.

Top-down ownership

All went out of their way to demonstrate to their customers and their teams that they were prepared to dig into payment data and go visit a company paying late, however large.

Mike's chemicals SME, whose very existence was at stake, had a leader prepared to wine and dine customer finance personnel who admitted they had never before been taken to lunch and who thereafter responded favourably to payment requests.

Bill said he talked to customer leaders who often simply did not know invoices had not been paid.

Peter built solid relationships with clients and was able to leverage those relationships highly effectively when payment delays occurred.

Each demonstrated a clear commitment to the customer – and in time this level of ownership cascaded to the sales team (see below) and the leadership were able to step back, track the data and only step in when needed.

Clear terms

A large company selling a complex mix of products and services needs to have the precise details of the deal recorded clearly and if necessary, for large deals, signed off by a bid committee.

The written terms need to cover what's being provided and when revenue recognition will be triggered.

For Amazon Papyrus, a detailed order which clearly specifies payment terms is enough, provided of course that the importance of sticking to agreed terms has been clearly laid out before supply begins.

Discrepancies and safety culture

Finding out where you went wrong is critical to removing obstacles to payment. This does not happen in a culture where mistakes are punished. Whenever an issue is unearthed, it must be addressed openly without fear of retribution. Unearthing it in time to prevent late payment may require proactive service – we advocate a formal process of early customer contact by phone or in person or (increasingly) via digital means to surface any unmet expectations early in the process and well before invoice due date.

Sales culture

All companies moved eventually to sales bonuses predicated on prompt invoice payment.

In each case, before triggering this they went through a process of sales education, both of a conceptual nature (basic balance sheet) and on practical issues like tracking performance and talking to customers about invoices.

Despite some salesmen losing bonuses due to inaction, all companies stuck firmly to this policy and regularly refresh the training.

Digital word

People sell to people, and people pay people, says Mike. Datacraft and Amazon Papyrus – one itself a technology company – progressively invested in better technology to track and measure customer interactions, order details, payment performance and sales collections effectiveness, but Mike and Bill both stressed the need for personal interaction.

Notably, neither of them see technology as a catch-all solution to on-time payment. Both stress intimacy through direct customer interaction at all stages and at the highest level.

Other insights

Interestingly, Bill spoke to the way that looking at quote-to-cash helped create a margin waterfall showing where leakage occurred.

For Amazon Papyrus, a less complex business with higher gross margins but a leaner balance sheet, getting paid was an existential issue.

For Datacraft, the health of quote-to-cash was and is a key indicator of relationship health and a leading measure of profitability.

For ModuResources, Peter sees the need for greater intimacy throughout the relationship as a key growth and retention tool in a time of great competitive pressure.

For Peter, VRC-driven intimacy has not only cut DSO in half but has also been a key differentiator in a competitive industry dominated and led by technical specialists.

The interviews in this chapter can be found in full at RIABU.com

Part 4
Into action

Your new service solution:
The Virtuous Revenue Cycle

Recap of your challenge

Companies that routinely get paid late by customers often live in a world of negativity. They spend lots of time chasing overdue transactions.

Fig. 4.1 - TYPICAL RECEIVABLES AGING BEFORE PROACTIVITY - NOTICE SUBSTANTIAL ROLLOVER

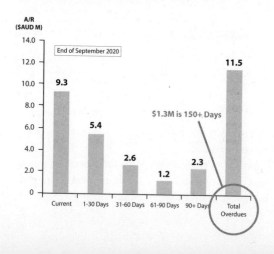

This shows a large number of invoices in the "rollover" (0–30 days) column, and other overdues in the 60, 90 and 90-plus columns.

In this situation, which is very common, most daily discussions with customers are about late invoices and are therefore uncomfortable and even adversarial, because of unmet expectations on both sides.

Internally, things are no better. The cash flow and DSO numbers are not right, issues remain long unresolved, and there's plenty of blame to go around.

The myths listed in Part 2.2 may now be widely used to assign responsibility elsewhere.

Often the finance department may feel especially frustrated because though the head of finance may well have receivables performance in his metrics, he has probably found that many of the causes of – and solutions to – timely payment are in practice outside his control.

Salesmen are uncomfortable being asked to broach the subject of late invoices with customers as, when they do, they are given details of unresolved issues which may have been occurring for a long time. This allows blame to be shifted away from sales.

Leadership is frustrated by the growing cash gap and the lack of clarity around what exactly has gone wrong and who is to be held accountable.

The problem of "negative modality"

Expressed in process terms, the reactive receivables environment looks like Figure 4.2:

Fig. 4.2 - TYPICAL AR BEFORE PROACTIVE INTRODUCTION

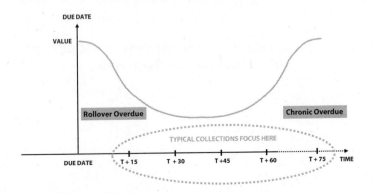

In this (very common) situation, all discussion about payment begins only *after* the payment is late.

Most companies that want to be paid contact customers after their payments are already late. This tends to make customer conversations uncomfortable – they know why you are calling.

By waiting until a problem already exists, you have created a specific modality for all customer discussions – a reactive modality, which is negative.

Today, the vast majority of the solutions on offer for AR management are specifically aligned to this negative modality, including:

- Dunning letters (letters pursuing overdue invoices)
- Automated reminders
- Lawyer's letters
- Debt collectors
- Arbitration

The problem of complexity – meet Vilfredo Pareto

From:
All customers are equally important and we therefore treat them the same.

To:
We prioritise customers who give us 80% of our sales or are problematic, and engage with them early and often so they get the very best service.

At this point you should already see that to be first in line to get paid, you may well need to make some big changes to the way you conduct customer relationships.

If you have a lot of customers – hundreds, perhaps thousands – the scale of the task may seem daunting and disheartening.

There is a solution, which will help you focus your efforts so as to get the fastest return on your efforts.

The Pareto principle

Early in the 20th century, an Italian economist called Vilfredo Pareto observed that all organisations behaved in certain predictable ways.

Fig. 4.3 - MEET VILFREDO PARETO

80% of results come from 20% of effort / time.

Vilfredo Pareto
Corso di Economia Politica

He suggested that by understanding and leveraging these patterns, politicians would be able to create maximum impact from economic policy and from the way they selectively deployed resources.

He laid out some simple rules that are a big help to businesses, because they can simplify what look like enormous tasks and help you to focus your efforts where you can have most effect.

The 80/20 rule

Probably most people have heard of Pareto's 80/20 rule, which (by extension from politics to commerce) states that 20% of your customers (the top 20% by sales value) are responsible for 80% of your receivables. Sort them out, and you have got 80% of your cash in on time.

If the top 20% of your customers give you 80% of sales, it follows that the remaining 80% of customers give you 20%.

All customers are important, but we suggest you invest in high-intensity proactive service for your top 20%. Since getting this up and running takes time and effort, you can start at the top (top 10% first) and work down.

Fig. 4.4 - PARETO RECEIVABLES TEMPLATE

Report Date:			Volume				Value			
Value Range			Volume of Customers	Cumulative Volume	%	Cum %	Value of A/R	Cumulative Volume	%	Cum %
	Over	1,000,000		-				-		
500,000	to	999,999		-				-		
250,000	to	499,999		-				-		
100,000	to	249,999		-				-		
50,000	to	99,999		-				-		
25,000	to	49,999		-				-		
10,000	to	24,999		-				-		
5,000	to	9,999		-				-		
2,500	to	4,999		-				-		
-	to	2,499		-				-		
Sub-Total				-				-		
Credit										
Total				-				-		

Stop when you have 80% of Receivables

Build your customer Pareto

List your customers in descending order of value. Your accounting system should be able to do this for you, but even if you need to use a spreadsheet it is not hard, and to help you get started we have included a Pareto template with the formulae you need already embedded.

Using the template, keep adding customers until you get to a cumulative 50% of sales. That is your top 10% – let us call them Tier 1 targets – and you can start with them.

Carry on further until you have reached 80% of sales and now you have Tier 2, the next 10% of customers who account for the next 30% of sales.

With Tiers 1 and 2, you have now listed 20% of your customers by number who account for 80% of your sales by value.

What remain are the 80% of customers – much smaller ones – who contribute 20% of sales. They constitute Tier 3 in our new terminology.

We will not forget them either, but we will focus to begin with on the top 2 tiers because by fixing them you will have fixed 80% of the problem of late payment in your business.

Add in the risky ones

You may want to make another list of the customers who make a habit of paying you late – large or small – as there are things you can do to bring them into line too, and you certainly do not want to ignore them. We will call them Tier 3.

Why make this list?

Because this list of your top 20% of customers represents 80% of your sales, it should guide you as you build your VRC.

Starting with these customers, apply all the principles in the VRC – ensure each has a signed credit policy, accurate and prompt invoices, and gets proactive contact using your new process.

If you have a great many customers, you can start with the top 10% (Tier 1) then move to the next 10% (Tier 2).

By proceeding in this way, you maximise the service and cash impact of the changes you are making!

In this chapter we will guide you in building a service intensity matrix to help you manage all the elements of receivables management, proactive and reactive.

Fig. 4.5 - SERVICE INTENSITY MATRIX

Customer Segment	Proactive Phone Contact	Selective Proactive Phone Contact	Reactive Phone Contact	Monthly Billing Statement	Dunning Letters
Tier 1	✓		✓	✓	
Tier 2		✓	✓	✓	
Tier 3				✓	✓
High Risk Accounts		✓	✓	✓	
Chronic Overdue Accounts Clean-up			✓	✓	✓

Figure 4.5 contains all the key elements. Do not worry if some elements are unclear, they will be by the end of this chapter.

Other useful examples of the Pareto

Pareto principles will help you prioritise customers, but note these other helpful uses of the Pareto:

- 20% of customer orders will deliver 80% of invoices by value (so make sure these are accurate!)
- 20% of invoices add up to 80% of revenue
- 20% of customers will be responsible for 80% of overdue invoices by value
- 20% of invoice errors ("discrepancies") will cause 80% of payments held up by uncorrected discrepancies
- 20% of discrepancy types will cause 80% of discrepancies

Implications

In business, especially in times of disruption and stress when resources may become more limited, the sheer volume of work can seem daunting.

These mathematical relationships should show you that careful focus can help you zero in on the things you need to fix first.

Always keep Mr Pareto close at hand, especially when you or your team are under stress and short of time.

Do

- Learn about the Pareto by analysing your customers in Pareto terms.
- Ensure that in addition to listing the big (top 20%) of customers you start to build a database of:
- Customers who habitually pay late
- Customers where sales intelligence or credit checks suggest there might be a looming problem
- Get your team comfortable with these concepts by having each functional lead explore the impacts of a Pareto analysis in his own area.
- Get sales leaders to report on the customers who deliver 80% of revenue in their individual portfolios and talk about ways to treat them differently.

Do not

- Trial any new process on your very largest and most important customers – reduce the risks of learning through trial and error by starting with less important customers.
- Try to boil the ocean by making changes to all customers at the same time.
- Treat all customer needs in the same way – you will need to keep an eye on this.

In due course, you should be able to take these principles and devise a tiered service environment which provides proactive contact with Tiers 1 and 2 and reactive to the rest. The table shows some of the things you need to think about as you build your new proactive service model.

4.1 Top-down ownership

Savvy leaders know that however compelling their product and however successful their marketing and sales team, they do not have a business at all if all their invoices do not get paid on time.

In our three case studies in the previous section, this simple wisdom is repeatedly stressed by the leaders we interviewed.

And a business that is growing fast where customer payments are also lengthening will experience an *exponential* growth in working capital; this widely unappreciated dynamic is the single biggest cause of business insolvency bar none in the world.

A leader who promotes the Virtuous Revenue Cycle constantly sends a "service and profitability" message to his team (later we will see how this can be enabled by shared KPIs and incentives, and by moving away from purely functional or silo goals):

- He is always willing to engage with the customer – or prospect – on service and payment (see case studies).
- He promotes the cross-functional ownership of profit, payment and service outcomes.
- He recognises the role of balance sheet discipline in achieving healthy financial outcomes. Getting lots of sales is not enough if customers do not pay on time.
- He insists that messages about payment discipline be routinely coded into all customer interactions, from the very beginning as part of a "We are a professional organisation and we do what we say, and we are thrilled to do business with companies like yours, who share the same values" message.
- He instils a culture of openness, where customer challenges or concerns, as well as internal dysfunction, can be aired and addressed without fear of criticism and retribution – this is no small thing in some cultures.

Team learns from leader
These key messages about the fundamental importance of being paid on time, and the link with service, are then carried and reinforced by the commercial team.

They are now a key part of your overall offering, through the order capture and fulfilment process, through billing, proactive customer service and reliable issue resolution.

Encouraging your team to get comfortable with an "elevator pitch" and regularly practising this at internal meetings is a good and fun way to ensure that your values percolate throughout your organisation.

We have met a number of leaders who – when a customer complained to them directly because they had been asked to pay an invoice that was due – agreed to a delay.

This undermined the rest of the team and ensured that payment terms would never again be taken seriously by that customer. And probably the service team would hesitate before pressing customers in future for fear of further interventions.

A leader must hold the line, or all is lost!

Stop-start programmes without lasting benefits

Receivables programmes born out of desperation often put abrupt pressure on customers to pay faster. Staff are coerced into pressing for payment.

But absent the service focus that lies at the heart of this book, programmes like this invariably create a toxic dynamic of short-term improvement, long-term relationship damage.

Without the correct VRC foundations, DSO will typically start to grow again after a brief period of improvement, whilst the customer feels uncomfortable if not aggrieved.

4.2 Clear credit policy

From:
We prefer to focus customer interactions on innovation and new sales; invoices always get paid eventually.

To:
As a professional organisation, we take pride in clearly defining (and meeting) all our customer commitments and expect our customers to do the same in return.

What is a credit policy?

A credit policy is a short document that sets out, in writing, how you will do business with your customer. It stipulates clearly and unambiguously what you will do for them and what they will do for you.

It includes important details like how you will invoice them, how you will deal with discrepancies, and what your payment terms are.

The idea is that you have a written policy for every customer and you both go through it and sign it before you start to do business.

What is your credit policy now?

Do you have a credit policy? Have your customers signed up to it?

This might seem like a foolish question but try asking your leadership team what agreed customer payment terms are, for specific accounts.

That is, ask them: "By precisely what day after invoice, or delivery, do we expect this customer's payment to be in our bank account?"

The answers you get will tell you a lot about the quality of your AR processes.

Check around. Ask your financial director, ask the salesman, check what your invoice says, ask the customer, and do not be surprised if you get blank looks or several different answers.

I met companies who gave me six different answers, depending on who I asked or where I looked.

The terms written in the computer customer master file, on the invoice, on the order, in the opinion of the salesman, in the opinion of the customer, and finally how long it actually takes for the customer's money to land in the bank... If you have multiple versions of your payment terms, you really have no terms at all.

For in reality (and sometimes even in law), if a customer has routinely been paying you "late" for a sustained period he can argue that the de facto payment term is the term he has been using – meaning that your original contractual terms have become whatever terms the customer has awarded himself!

Why do you need a credit policy?

No lasting improvement in customer payments is possible unless you have a firm contractual foundation with each and every customer for each and every transaction which stipulates (in addition to important details of product or service quality, order lead times, etc.) precisely when you expect to be paid and how payments may be made.

If you are confident that you already have clearly defined terms of trade, agreed in writing, with every customer, then you may want to move on to the next chapter.

If not, then follow the steps required for how to benchmark, model and set terms, how to build internal alignment across your team, how to ensure that new customers stick to your terms, and – much harder! – how to move established customers to *your* terms rather than theirs.

You need a credit policy you are serious about, because without it you have no formal basis for creating internal or external discipline around receivables and remain at the mercy of your customers when it comes to getting paid.

A simple credit policy
If you are a substantial entity, you will already have a credit policy; it may well run to many pages, including much lawyerly language.

Such a detailed policy can be found in Part 9, but for smaller entities who want to get started, here is a simple example.

Fig. 4.6 - CREDIT POLICY
Here is a simple example of a credit policy which should be fully endorsed by yourself and your leadership team and then signed by your customer

(Name of your company) ... credit policy
Provided to (name of customer or prospective customer)

Purpose of this document
This document describes our professional commitment to you, our customer, and is intended to ensure that we always meet the highest standards in our relationship, which is based on mutual respect.

Service commitment
· We take pride in providing you our customer with prompt and responsive service, and in adhering to commitments made on quality, timeliness, and accuracy.
· For this reason we will periodically refresh and re-send our Credit Policy, so that we remain aligned as our relationship grows.
· We want our relationship to run smoothly, so that we can prosper and grow.
· We ask that you provide us with the names and contact details of your key staff so we can quickly reach out to them to identify and settle any service or product issues.

Payment term
Your agreed payment term is....
· Price and payment terms are part of our mutual commitment to excellence.
· These terms of payment, once agreed, should be adhered to by both parties and cannot be varied except by prior written agreement.
· A term of payment defines the date upon which full payment should be received in our bank account.

Orders, invoices, payments
· All customer orders will state price, delivery date, and agreed payment terms
· We will invoice you promptly once you have received your delivery, and invoices will include agreed payment terms
· Shortly after you have received your invoice we will call to check that all is in order
· Should you report a delivery or invoice discrepancy, we will work hard to resolve it quickly
· If the invoice is in order, we will request that you confirm that you will make payment on the agreed payment terms

Discrepancies
· You will undertake to advise us promptly of any issues or discrepancies
· The name and contact details of our Customer Service Staff can be found on your invoice
· Should you be unable to reach the staff named on the invoice you may call this free number........

Stop order policy
· Should an invoice or invoices become significantly overdue where there is no known discrepancy we may decline to accept further orders
· Please ensure you pay to terms so this can be avoided
· This (stop order) action would be taken with the greatest reluctance
· We hope that you, our valued customer, will follow the policies laid out here so we can continue to provide uninterrupted service to you

Other conditions
Other undertakings are stated in the attached legal terms. Signature of this document implies acceptance of these undertakings and the attached terms.

Signed and accepted

Establishing the right terms
In setting the right terms, you will need to look at generally accepted practice in your geography and sector.

See also Part 2 on how to take into account risk when you determine what terms to offer.

Model your balance sheet so that whatever terms you adopt will, based on forecast sales and customer mix, lead to a cash outcome that will:

- Pay the bills and keep the lights on
- Generate cash for investment
- Keep external borrowing needs to a manageable level.

Sometimes your own team – anxious not to "challenge" customers – may campaign for longer terms on the basis of "market conditions" or "aggressive competitors" or other external or historical factors. Resist! If you give in at an early stage, you will struggle to get anywhere and instead create a damaging precedent.

Above all, do not commit to a substantial new customer without ensuring that you are able to fund any additional working capital implied by the credit terms you are being asked to agree. (As a rule of thumb, if the customer terms you are considering are longer than your current BPDSO, the impact of the new customer will be negative – your DSO will grow even if you get paid on time.)

We look in detail at how you can track this using BPDSO in Part 5.

Later on, you will also learn some practical ways to get your own team to see the need for strict terms, and some tools to help them position and communicate this need to their customers.

Making policy matter

However elegant your written credit policy, it is worthless unless it is supported by your team, communicated to customers, and properly adhered to by *both*.

For this reason, the longer your written policy, the less likely it will be taken seriously – so consider putting key commercial terms up front and any detailed legalese in attachment.

The first step, therefore, once you are clear about the terms you want to offer customers (see also Part 5), is to iron out any internal disagreements and ensure that your own leadership team understands and agrees with your policy.

They must then ensure that their functional teams, in turn, are fully comfortable. This may take a bit of time but it will be time well spent if it prevents misalignment later.

To do this, you may want to start by defining to your team in clear terms the financial impact to the company of getting paid late and also provide some compelling examples of why this happens and how often.

Above all, you must stress that everyone owns working capital and that it is vital that you and your team *all* speak with one voice to the customer.

The second step is to ensure that your customers are on board and this will typically require that you:

- Coach your account managers on how to broach this issue with customers, with role-play if necessary
- Keep track of progress as you/they confirm terms with customers, and make sure you log and respond to any pushback
- For large customers, ensure that terms are formally confirmed face-to-face by senior account managers
- For smaller accounts, send a friendly letter reminding them what their terms of payment are
- Pay attention to pushback and where necessary iron out differences in a cool and calm fashion
- Never walk away from a discussion on terms where the customer is clearly unhappy and unconvinced – this ensures trouble later on

Steps

1. Use performance data on overdues to establish the need for a disciplined and consistent policy.
2. Take the simple credit policy template we provide or use the more detailed one in the appendix and discuss each element internally.
3. To define desired payment terms, look at the market and, if necessary, use external benchmarks.
4. Ensure all members of your team sign off on the agreed terms and policy.
5. Ensure the formal policy is shared with customers and signed off by them.
6. Consider sales coaching to help your team with this process – especially if you judge that, from force of habit, they may give mixed messages to their customers.
7. Regularly review feedback and progress, promote peer learning, acknowledge and encourage "luminaries".

Do

- Check out how many different terms you are offering customers.
- Check out how many versions of your payment terms exist – on paper and in people's minds.
- If upon enquiry you find there may be many terms, then research and list them because this baseline will be essential for planning and driving change.
- Seek real data on what terms your competitors are offering – from a credible source, not anecdotes from your team or elsewhere, and not other customers who have an obvious incentive to persuade you to be lenient and let them pay later.
- Engage your team in developing your credit policy, allowing time to explore and overcome objections, and build alignment.
- Limit the number of different terms you grant to future customers,

and carefully control permitted exceptions by having a formal sign-off process.
- Include in your analysis examples of customer discrepancies and how long it takes to resolve them.
- Model payment terms using BPDSO (see part 1) so your team can understand how differing customer and terms mixes can dramatically influence your working capital requirement.
- Make clear rules regarding desired customer terms, the need to limit exceptions, and the authorisation process for doing so.
- Ensure you review your agreed credit policy annually, or when changes in the market (recession, an aggressive competitor, etc.) require.
- If you have many customers, you may want to (re)confirm terms in face-to-face meetings with the biggest 20% of customers, and by letter with remaining customers.

Do not
- Allow anecdotal evidence – "This is what we are hearing in the market, this is what people say"– to sway you from your purpose.
- Give in to blackmail from doomsayers who claim that firming up terms will lose you business. Good customers will pay on time and others may not be economically desirable.
- Permit functional heads to dissent from the agreed policy (watch out for unstated and unaddressed objections). Once the analysis and debate are finished, the policy that emerges must be a common team position.
- Grant a plethora of terms to different customers. Have as few terms as possible, and manage exceptions rigorously.
- Grant different terms to different branches, or departments, of the same company – they will inevitably find out and everyone will insist on moving to the longest term you have granted.

4.3 Prompt and accurate invoicing

The single commonest reason for late payment is an error or omission on the invoice. I have been amazed to receive invoices that stipulated payment terms but did not explain where the payment should be sent (no bank details) or – more commonly – made no mention of payment terms or due date at all.

Accuracy
An accurate invoice is key to getting paid – so make sure you are armed

with the critical customer information, from the very start, that you need to create a perfect invoice.

When you share your credit policy with your customer, you should be armed with a list of things that you need to know if you are to meet their documentary and service requirements and get paid.

Some of these things are obvious – like where to send the delivery, the precise name of the company, etc.

But in order to have a Virtuous Revenue Cycle with a customer, you will need to know a lot more about how they are organised and how they operate.

Fig. 4.7 - TYPICAL PROCURE-TO-PAY JOURNEY

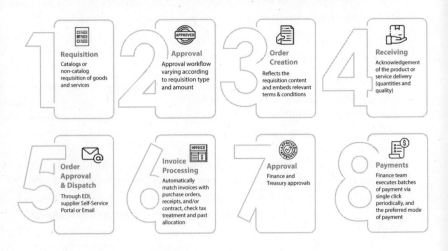

The simplest way to think about it is that each customer has a process for:

- Selecting a supplier
- Contracting
- Making an order
- Receiving a delivery or service
- Confirming a delivery or service
- Receiving an invoice
- Validating an invoice
- Dealing with invoice discrepancies
- Assigning the invoice for payment
- Approving an invoice for payment
- Paying the invoice

Once you have completed your credit policy and it is signed, you should have all the details you need to create a clean invoice and maintain contact with the right customer staff to ensure that your invoice is approved and paid.

You may want to use the customer mapping template – Fig 4.8 – or something similar to capture key customer contact data for service purposes.

Fig. 4.8 - CUSTOMER MAPPING TEMPLATE FOR PROACTIVE SERVICE CALLS

mer name	Debtor #	Sales Rep	BU	Region	First Service Call (Engineer)			Courtesy/Reminder Calls (Payables)			Process Overview			
					Single contact point Y/N	Contact Point(s)	Suggested time for contact (mth/day)	Single point of contact Y/N	Contact Point(s)	Suggested time for contact (mth/day)	Who receives invoice?	Who approves?	Who organises payment?	(Who raises discrepancies?)

Description — Comprehensive mapping of customer contact information and payment approval processes facilitates effective proactive calling by customer service. | Understanding of customer's payment approval process helps to motivate the customer's engineer, site manager or procurement manager to approve invoice for payment, or to pass invoice on for approval.

It is true that in a very small company, one or two people may actually do all these things. But even in a medium-sized SME there might easily be 5–10 people involved in all these activities.

In order to have a perfect invoice, you have to meet the requirements of each of these steps (see Fig 4.7), so before you start doing business you need to know:

- What are the customer requirements for each step? Is there a written process?
- If they have an automated supplier management system, how can you get set up?
- Who is in charge of each step (name, title, email, phone)?
- For each department or function involved, who is the line manager?
- How long does each step typically take?

This is a very long list!

In reality your invoice could get stuck *anywhere* in this process and it may be hard to find out where it is stuck unless you know in advance the way your customer operates and can track the payment transaction step by step.

You need to know *all* of this before you start doing business, and the time to get the details is when you are discussing price, payment, etc., at the beginning. Relations at this stage are generally cordial, details are being ironed out.

Collecting these key data later on, when you are struggling to free up an overdue invoice, may be much, much harder.

If you let the customer deflect you and you go ahead and supply him without knowing these details about how they operate, then you will find it hard to manage your service and collections process.

It may take months before you are a completely clear about who does what in your customer's payment process, and where you can get hold of them. By that time, you may have a considerable pile of overdue invoices.

When you start to introduce the VRC and you make your first proactive calls (this is one reason why we suggested you roll out the new process progressively rather than all at once), you are likely to discover very quickly customers who have issues with your invoices.

These issues are likely to include some requirements you knew about (or should have known about), like the ones listed above, but failed to meet, and also some new ones that not only did you not meet but which you were unaware of and which may in some cases seem exigent and unreasonable.

Sometimes it takes time to tease out the complete list of requirements from your customer – by "forgetting" to communicate certain requirements your customer may have created speed bumps allowing the transaction to be delayed.

Some business consultants advise their clients to make their payment processes complicated solely to make it easier to hang on longer to their payment.

It is your job to tease out all the wrinkles so that there are no defensible reasons for holding up payment and your perfect invoice can be paid promptly.

Never mind that this delaying behaviour (and the customer's related criticisms) may sometimes seem deliberate and unreasonable. Always take him at his word, remain scrupulously polite, and begin the process of creating the perfect invoice.

Timely revenue recognition – or when should we invoice?

For many of you, cutting an invoice occurs straight after you deliver your good or service. The timing is clear.

But for some industries with more complex business models, the question of when exactly to send an invoice and what to include in it is a vexed issue – check out the first of our case studies where a complex mix of hardware and services need to be billed and collections issues arise.

Often, as Bill relates in our first case study, when the terms of your contract are not defined precisely enough, the customer can find room to decline payment.

- When should goods and services be delivered?
- What precisely are those goods and services?
- What are the customer acceptance criteria which need to be met before the invoice can be prepared?
- What form of customer acceptance do we need to get to enable us to invoice (signature, email etc)?

When you cannot bill because acceptance criteria have not been met, you have (in effect) created a further delay which adds to your working capital needs in the form of "unbilled revenue".

Do
- Ensure that, where relevant, every customer contract defines clear revenue recognition terms:
  - At what stages in the delivery cycle can you bill?
  - What objectives need to be met for an invoice to be issued?
  - What is the customer sign-off process (strongly recommended!)?
- Ensure that getting these customer data becomes a standard part of customer onboarding, carried out at the same time as getting your credit policy signed.
- Ensure that your account managers (salesmen and women) understand why this is important and back up the request for information as and when necessary.
- Get these data *before* you start doing business.
- Regularly enquire when calling or visiting your customer whether any contact details have changed.
- Make a point of meeting customer staff in person if at all possible. If you can, get your sales account manager to introduce your service staff too.
- For key customer contacts, make it a habit to check in with them to ensure things are okay – and find out their birthdays.

Do not
- Go ahead with supply without these details.
- Let your account manager deflect responsibility – you may need a training session on this.
- Wait for a problem to arise with the delivery, service or invoice before finding out names and contact details – this guarantees delayed payment.
- Be deflected – ever – from getting the information you need from your customer to get paid on time. It is an entirely reasonable expectation on your part to be given it, and a new customer who seems reluctant to divulge these data should be treated with care, as he may be laying the groundwork for payment delay.

4.4 Proactive customer service model

The key to changing the modality of customer interactions from reactive and negative to proactive and positive lies in *leading with service*, well before the invoice is even due.

This may require a significant change in the way you approach customers and therefore needs to be properly thought through and communicated to your customers before you introduce any actual changes.

The objective of this early contact is to remove any obstacles to timely payment and, over time, to change your receivables aging profile to the one in Fig 4.9.

Fig. 4.9 - TYPICAL AR PROFILE AFTER PROACTIVE INTRODUCTION

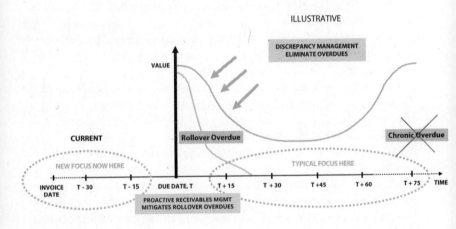

Set-up

Using the Pareto template (Fig 4.4) you completed earlier, inform the top 20% of your customers that they will be receiving enhanced dedicated service (we have added some examples of letters or emails you might use to do this in the appendix). If 20% is more than you can handle with the team you have, start with the top 10% (Tier 1).

- Have the account manager confirm this new service face-to-face with Tier 1 accounts.
- Follow it up in writing.
- Write to other (non-Tier 1) accounts.

Next, create a collections activity log to ensure you plan and track contact with these customers in a methodical way and meticulously follow up.

Fig. 4.10 - COLLECTIONS ACTIVITY LOG - A SUGGESTION
The log should contain next steps and a specific follow up date

Debtor No.	SEM222		Customer Name	ELECTROLUX WASHER DIVISION			
Debtor No.	Invoice No.	Invoice Date	Invoice Amount	Comments/Actions Taken	Date	Follow-up Required	Due Date
5EM222	6313363	10/1/2020	1,622.50	Electrolux not aware of overdue invoice. Payment expected 25/10/2020	20/10/20		25/10/20

Debtor No.	5RE608		Customer Name	RESOLVE FM (Wrong customer refer DL)			
Debtor No.	Invoice No.	Invoice Date	Invoice Amount	Comments/Actions Taken	Date	Follow-up Required	Due Date
5RE608	653712	2/21/2020	1,119.36	Wrong customer. Invoice is for work completed prior to October 2020 when resolve started work at Adelaide Brighton Cement. Invoice redirected to Adelaide Brighton Cement	20/10/20	Awaiting e-mail response from Adelaide Brignton Cement	25/10/20
5RE608	653713	2/21/2020	1,119.36	Wrong customer. Invoice is for work completed prior to October 2020 when resolve started work at Adelaide Brighton Cement. Invoice redirected to Adelaide Brighton Cement	20/10/20	Awaiting e-mail response from Adelaide Brignton Cement	25/10/20

Debtor No.	5GE300		Customer Name	GENERAL MOTORS HOLDEN AUTOMOT			
Debtor No.	Invoice No.	Invoice Date	Invoice Amount	Comments/Actions Taken	Date	Follow-up Required	Due Date
5GE300	614852	6/24/2020	4,356.00	Wrong purchase order number on invoice, needs to be reissued with Purchase Order number WY01577, Holden sending e-mail confirming location to send adjusted invoice to.	21/10/20	Awaiting e-mail response from customer	25/10/20

Description: Collection activities for long overdue accounts should be tracked and each conversation logged

To ensure you are meeting their expectations, a customer service specialist should contact them weekly soon after invoicing to ensure that:

- Recent deliveries have met standards of quality and timeliness
- Delivery and invoicing documentation is accurate and compliant
- There are no outstanding concerns or issues on this or other outstanding transactions
- Any earlier discrepancies are adequately resolved

Fig.4.11 - PROACTIVE COLLECTIONS CALLS SEND A DIFFERENT MESSAGE THAN PAST DUE COLLECTIONS CALLS, AND SPEAKING WITH CUSTOMERS REGULARLY ENHANCES THE OVERALL RELATIONSHIP

Proactive calling signals the company's intention to move towards a more customer focused program and to provide better service to customers

The more the company knows about customers, the easier it is to assist them with any problems and gain assurance that they are able to pay all invoices in full

Every time you speak with our customers, there is the opportunity to:

- Make a thorough review of their account

- Update any changes

- Assist them with any problems that would be cause for non-payment

The goal of successful telephone contact is to build and maintain a good working relationships (i.e. get invoices paid as early as possible)

Ensure you establish whether there are any gaps or errors in the documentation, including the invoice.

If there are discrepancies, politely record them, assign a ticket number, and commit to resolve them within a specific timeframe.

If the invoice has been checked and there are no discrepancies, you may then politely reconfirm the payment terms included in your invoice and written in the agreed credit policy for that customer.

You may politely ask for confirmation that those terms will be met and agree what the precise payment due date is and how their internal process works.

If you already know their internal payment processes – and the names and contact details of who does what (you should!) – check for recent changes anyway because processes, and people, change.

By asking in the right way – you want to make sure things go smoothly – you again demonstrate your professionalism and ensure you do not waste time in future contacting the wrong individual.

Steps
1. Develop a written script for your proactive calling process.
2. Build your discrepancy management process in parallel (next chapter) and have it ready before you start proactive calling.
3. Conduct internal training on the new call process.
4. Let customers know about your enhanced service process.
5. Trial the process with a few customers first and strengthen or adjust as required.
6. Once it is effective, quickly scale up to cover your top 20% of customers.

Do
- Remember that a "proactive" call soon after invoicing is *not* a collections call. It is a customer service call.
- Ensure that the right language is used internally when setting this up. Terms like "collections," "chasing the customer", etc., must be avoided as you build awareness of what real proactive service looks like.
- Advise all major customers ahead of time – if possible, face-to-face – that you are investing in an enhanced service capability that will include early phone contact designed to ensure that they are getting the service they expect.
- Ensure you have the full support of your sales team and that they understand the service value of this innovation.
- Develop a customer checklist before starting proactivity. Check that the customer has signed the credit policy, been introduced to the new proactive service idea, and that if he expressed any concerns these have been dealt with.

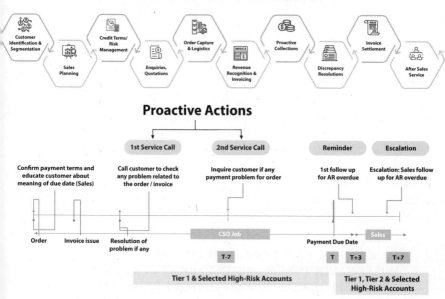

Fig. 4.12 - TO GET PAID ON TIME, AGREE TERMS AND DUE DATE, AND INITIATE PROACTIVE CALLING

Do not

- Start proactive service calls without agreeing the process with your own sales team.
- Test proactive calls with your biggest, most important accounts. Start with the bottom of your top 20% until you get the process right.
- Launch proactive service calls without introducing this new enhanced service to customers, face-to-face to big accounts.
- Launch proactive service calls without completing your checklist.
- Launch any proactive calls until you have in place a robust and explicitly agreed internal process for dealing promptly with any discrepancies that may come up.

Now that you have identified the customers who are critical and started engaging with them early, you should create a matrix to ensure you are addressing each customer appropriately given their size and risk. Go back to Figure 4.5, which should now be clearer.

4.5 Prompt discrepancy resolution

From:
When we hear about discrepancies, we try and handle them as best we can, but everybody is busy.

To:
The whole team identifies and captures all unmet customer expectations as early as possible after billing; we resolve them quickly and track our responsiveness.

Figure 4.13 captures the components of an effective discrepancy management process which "integrates" the various functions concerned with identifying, capturing and resolving discrepancies.

Fig. 4.13 - IDM: A SUCCESSFUL COLLECTIONS ENVIRONMENT MUST INCLUDE THE CAPABILITY TO IDENTIFY, CAPTURE AND PROMPTLY RESOLVE "UNMET CUSTOMER EXPECTATIONS"

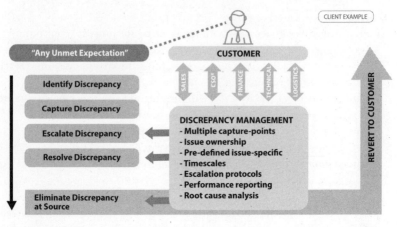

* Customer Service Officer

Be ready to correct mistakes quickly
Companies that start making service calls to customers soon after invoicing using our approach are often surprised by how many times they are told about errors or omissions that, left uncorrected, would have delayed or even prevented payment.

Quite often, once you start this process you quickly find yourself with a big pile of invoice discrepancies, many of which are quite old.

Because you have not done it this methodical way in the past, you have remained unaware of just how many customer discrepancies there are.

If you get swamped by the unexpectedly large volume of "unmet expectations" uncovered by your new service process and are, as a result, unable to resolve them all promptly, then you will have created a whole new problem by raising customer expectations with a detailed announcement and not meeting them.

You need to avoid this at all costs, as negative customer feedback on your new proactive process is not just bad for customer relations but it will also provide sceptics within your own organisation with a reason to criticise the whole process.

Start slowly, learn as you go

For this reason, we suggest that you start by phoning only a few customers, and that you make sure that you are ready – really ready – to deal with their issues promptly and effectively when they raise them.

If you start asking customers – who may in some cases already be quite frustrated – to give you details of what needs to be corrected yet fail to make the corrections promptly because you are not (internally) ready, you run the risk of making a bad situation much worse by falsely raising expectations.

By the way, finding out about lots of unmet expectations is a good thing, not a bad thing, because it gives you the insight you need to make changes to the way you operate and improve your overall service delivery.

Start small, with one or two accounts managed by supportive salesmen, and only expand when you are satisfied that your calls are working *and* that you are able to respond to all the issues raised by those customers in a timely fashion.

Since responding to the customer in a timely fashion may require, for some issues, that other internal functions act, investigate and resolve them, and they may have grown used to taking their time over this, you will want to iron out these internal responsiveness issues before extending your new proactive process to all your customers.

To recap, you should:

- Make sure your customer understands the purpose of the new service process before launching it (ideally you should have introduced it when reviewing and signing the credit policy)
- Launch it with a few customers initially so you can test your approach – including the script – as well as your internal ability to respond quickly to discrepancies when they arise
- Revisit the script, resolution timescales and ownership before you start doing this for all of your top customers

To get payments on track you need to:
- Identify and log all issues as soon as they are reported by whoever they are reported to – the **Identifier**
- Ensure all issues are copied or forwarded to the **Service Coordinator**
- Assign each issue to a specific **Resolution Area**
- Attach an agreed response time (in days) to each issue by type
- When the response is received, revert to the customer (usually by the **Customer Service Coordinator**)
- If the response is *not* received automatically, escalate the issue to an **Escalation Area**

You may want to follow the sample flow chart below:

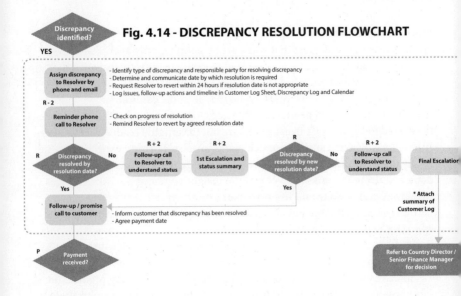

Fig. 4.14 - DISCREPANCY RESOLUTION FLOWCHART

Identifier

Up to now, it has mostly been the responsibility of our "collectors" to call customers and press for payment, taking note of unmet expectations when they arise and dealing with them as quickly as possible

But in reality, anyone on your team who interacts with a customer – from the CEO down, and including third parties like distributors – may hear about customer concerns.

These concerns may include specific problems with transactions, issues with responsiveness, or general gripes about individuals or processes.

Information about unmet expectations is gold, so all Identifiers (people who have learned of a customer concern) must record the issue and capture specific information.

INTO ACTION   107

Customer Service Coordinator

It makes sense to have an individual or function who maintains contact with the customer, makes calls as necessary, and monitors internal responses from Resolvers.

Having multiple points of contact increases the risk of delay, duplication or miscommunication, so we suggest that all discrepancies go through a Customer Service individual or team

Reminder: This is the person or function whose name and details are given to all customers, included in your credit policy and on invoices, *and* shared internally so that everyone knows who to phone or email when there is an issue.

This individual will:

- Call customers
- Track payment history
- Capture discrepancies
- Monitor resolution performance
- Ensure unresolved issues are escalated as necessary
- Keep track of recurring issues

Resolution Area (or Resolver)

A resolver is responsible for resolving a discrepancy and advising the Customer Service Coordinator what has been done.

Because the payment of an invoice often depends on a timely resolution, the Resolver must be the right person – the individual who has or can get the answer to the specific issue who must also commit to a target resolution timescale (in days) which will be communicated to the customer after the discrepancy has been surfaced.

With the Resolver, it is important that an *individual* is nominated, *not* a function ("sales") or an office ("HK depot"), as we will be measuring responsiveness and holding individuals accountable.

Companies vary greatly but these functions are likely to be sources for providing Resolvers:

- Distribution (Did it get there in full and on time?)
- Transport (Were the necessary signatures or receipt numbers procured?)
- Sales (Were the terms of sale, product price, etc., accurate?)
- Finance (Did we calculate correctly, e.g. FX rates?)
- IT (Did a data input error cause an invoice error?)

Obviously each company is slightly different so you need to list the types of discrepancy that you know occur and assign the right Resolvers for your situation.

Be ready to add and amend as required and as you learn more. As we have said, once you start talking to the customer more, you may be surprised what you learn.

Escalation Area (or Auditor)

In our new VRC world, we take service and responsiveness very seriously.

So although we take time to build our new service processes, consult everyone and get everyone aligned, once we get going we are resolved to hold individuals accountable for their responsiveness.

When you are a Resolver, you are required to respond to a raised issue promptly and within the pre-agreed timescale. If you do not, the whole process fails.

- Customer is let down
- Discrepancy is unresolved
- Invoice remains unpaid
- Company credibility and professionalism are damaged

For this reason, the final thing you need to do when setting this up is to nominate a senior individual who is alerted when discrepancies remain unresolved by the Resolver in the pre-agreed timescale.

For this important check to be meaningful, it is very likely that the Auditor will *not* be the line manager of the Resolver. This is because a line manager may sometimes be sympathetic to the views of the Resolver – who works for him and who he may know well.

A more effective solution therefore is to ensure that unresolved discrepancies get escalated to a senior manager to whom the Resolver does not report. This might be the CFO or another individual, depending of course on the size and structure of your company.

What is important is that service commitments made to the customer are met 100% and on time. There is absolutely no point in strengthening credit policy, increasing customer communication, and investing in early proactive content if after all this a customer issue emerges and is then not addressed in a timely and professional fashion.

Setting it up: Create an IDM template

By talking to your team and by checking recent billing adjustments, make a list of discrepancies that you know have occurred in the past.

Remember that we define a discrepancy as any unmet customer expectation. You will immediately see that when we use this definition, we give our customer permission to define his own expectations.

This is because to have a genuine VRC, we want to understand *every reason* he chooses to use for delaying payment. It also means that we can expect to discover some things we were not aware of, as well as some things that do not make sense to us or even seem unreasonable.

One client – a successful engineering company – termed every customer discrepancy a "non-compliance". The request from the customer could then be assessed against the written rules for each transaction and denied if no rule had specifically been broken.

This missed the entire point of the process, which is to get into the client's mind and find out what he is thinking, so as to change his thinking by being responsive to his needs and smoothing the path to payment.

Discovering things you need to know to get paid on time and make your processes more effective is always a good thing, never a bad thing.

Even if you have the impression that the customer could have told you sooner or is "pushing his luck" (say by always mysteriously losing the invoice!), always treat a discrepancy as a learning opportunity and remain civil and responsive.

Resolution areas and timescale

Once you have a list of recurring discrepancies, discuss internally which function is responsible for resolving each type of issue.

These functions may include finance, sales, supply chain, IT... it will depend on your business.

Each function must:

- Acknowledge their responsibility for resolving the specific discrepancy type
- Suggest a reasonable turnaround time, in days (watch out for attempts to de-prioritise by suggesting weeks or "end of the month")
- If the proposed response time is longer than 2 days, they must have a very good reason. This is a business priority, *not* something you turn to only when all other activities have been completed.

Remember, until they give their response you cannot even begin the process of making a correction and seeking payment.

You should have come up with a table that looks something like Figure 4.15.

You will see that in addition to assigning each type of discrepancy to a specific Resolution Area and giving it a Resolution Timescale" of 1–7 days, we have added an Escalation Area.

When you receive a discrepancy from a customer, you undertake to resolve it in the appropriate time-frame – as per your internal agreement.

If you fail to do this, you have:

- Broken your agreement with the customer
- Delayed the correcting of the error
- Delayed the payment of the invoice
- Made your new service promise look insincere

Fig. 4.15 - PROACTIVE CONTACT SHOULD NOT BE INITIATED UNTIL YOU HAVE IDENTIFIED DISCREPANCY TYPES AND AGREED RESOLUTION AREAS

DISCREPANCY TYPE	RESOLUTION AREA¹	RESPONSE TIME (DAYS)	1ST ESCALATION AREA	RESPONSE TIME (DAYS)	2ND ESCALATION AREA
Wrong product invoiced	CS	4	Site Mgr	10	Country Dir / BU Head
Wrong product delivered	CS	4	Site Mgr	10	Country Dir / BU Head
Wrong PO Number	CS	4	Site Mgr	10	Country Dir / BU Head
Expired PO Number	CA	4	Site Mgr	10	Country Dir / BU Head
Missing PO Number	S	4	District Mgr	10	Country Dir / BU Head
Wrong price	S	7	District Mgr	10	Country Dir / BU Head
Price increase disputed by customer	S	7	District Mgr	10	Country Dir / BU Head
Terms Not Agreed	S	7	District Mgr	10	Country Dir / BU Head
Customer has no funds	S	4	District Mgr	10	Country Dir / BU Head
Duplicate Invoice	CS	4	Site Mgr	10	Country Dir / BU Head
Wrong Site	CS	4	Site Mgr	10	Country Dir / BU Head
Wrong part number/pack size	CS	4	Site Mgr	10	Country Dir / BU Head
Late / delayed delivery	CS	4	Site Mgr	10	Country Dir / BU Head
No Proof of Delivery	CS	4	Site Mgr	10	Country Dir / BU Head
No service report	S	4	District Mgr	10	Country Dir / BU Head
Fuel surcharge not agreed/disputed	S	7	District Mgr	10	Country Dir / BU Head

> Discrepancies that are not remedied within the prescribed response time are escalated to management for additional action

For this reason, issues not resolved according to the pre-agreed time-frame go into a weekly escalation report which identifies overdue issues to the next level of management.

In due course, individuals will have their performance in responding to discrepancies for which they are responsible included in their performance reviews.

Other useful templates for effective IDM can be found in Part 9.

4.6 Systematic root cause elimination

From:
We deal with customer discrepancies as they arise.

To:
We methodically track unmet customer expectations and quickly make the changes necessary to ensure they stop happening.

Crafting the perfect invoice is a continuous process
I learned valuable lessons from a German client who took a binary approach to the order-to-cash process.

"All we want," he insisted, "is to produce the perfect invoice." I thought at the time that this sounded utopian – because requirements change constantly in an active business – but if you apply the "Be first in line to get paid" lens, this makes perfect sense.

As you delve into the reasons why payments get held up, you are likely to discover a heap of things that are missing or wrong from your billing process.

Many will seem quite trivial – for example certain data on the wrong part of the page – but the secret to being first in line to get paid lies in being very, very precise about details.

Your goal, as you move towards a Virtuous Revenue Cycle, should be to add what is missing and correct what is wrong. So that every time you begin a customer transaction, you are following a clearly laid-down process that minimises the possibility that there will need to be delay or rework.

A perfect invoice is an invoice that allows a solvent and honest customer no opportunity to delay your payment. To be perfect, your invoices need to align with customer requirements from the very start – even ones that the customer may not have actually divulged – and to be quickly adjusted to reflect any changes or additions that your new service process reveals or which the customer may make in the course of time.

Fig.4.16 - DURING PROACTIVE CONTACT, CAPTURE ALL CUSTOMER DISCREPANCIES; MAKE A LIST OF HOW OFTEN EACH DISCREPANCY TYPE OCCURS, AND WHAT "LOST REVENUE FACTOR" (LRF) IS ASSOCIATED WITH EACH DISCREPANCY TYPE

Use data from most recent three months | Jan 2021 - Mar 2021

NO.	TYPE OF DISCREPANCY	NO. OF TIMES OCCURRED	LOST REVENUE FACTOR (LRF), $
1	Material returned	59	25,000
2	Tax wrongly charged	11	15,000
3	Price wrongly charged	8	10,000
4	Discount not charged	6	37,000
5	Double invoicing	1	3,000
6	Over consumption	8	2,000
	TOTAL	93	$92,000

Having evidence of how much revenue is held up by each discrepancy type is helpful when getting internal support for process changes – and when we get to Part 7 you will see that this kind of hard data is also very helpful in building the case for changing to the VRC!

As your proactive calling evolves, you will collect a list of recurring discrepancies. Each will be dealt with in a timely manner based on the template in Fig 4.15.

But now you should take steps to eliminate the recurring discrepancies. See Fig 4.16 for a simple way to prioritise recurring discrepancy types by listing

- Type of discrepancy
- How often they occur (number in a period)
- Total value of invoices held up – we call this the Lost Revenue Factor or LRF

You can now examine what needs to change internally to prevent these types of discrepancy recurring.

By using the concept of LRF in your management meetings, you can create urgency and a clear list of priorities.

In the short term, eliminating the root cause of these costly lapses may take time but remember you are ensuring they *stop* happening so the future impact will be a reduction in service, sales and leadership time spent on resolving discrepancies to free up customer payments.

Fig. 4.17 - DISCREPANCY ROOT CAUSE ANALYSIS WILL HELP IDENTIFY AND PRIORITISE COST REDUCTION OPPORTUNITIES BY CUSTOMER…

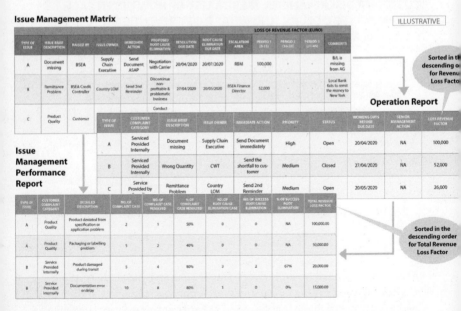

Figure 4.17 gives a snapshot of the kind of reports you can derive from IDM linked to proactive customer contact. You can track poor resolution performance – and in due course link it to pay – and you can measure causes and solutions.

Other examples of IDM reports can be found in the appendices in Part 9.

4.7 Engaged, motivated sales team

From:
Our sales team focuses on getting growth and having great customer relationships.

To:
Our sales team manages the entire customer relationship so as to maximise profitability service and cash.

Trying to change customer payment behaviour without the active support of your sales team is a fool's errand. No one plays a more critical role in the success of a commercial enterprise than the salesman or woman.

The salesperson is ambassador, technical expert, and often friend and entire counsel to his or her customer. Over time, they may become friends and mingle socially.

Since the salesman spends more time in contact with the customer – physically and virtually – than anyone else in your business, he almost certainly also has more influence with the customer than anyone else in your organisation.

Because of this pre-existing relationship, the salesman is the conduit for most communication to the customer, whom he may know well.

It follows that an initiative that seeks to make significant changes in the way the customer relationship is conducted – and gently adjust key aspects of customer behaviour – will struggle to succeed without the active support of the relationship manager.

For the VRC prescribed in this book to work effectively, your salesman will need to:

- Understand the critical importance of working capital, and the need to manage receivables effectively
- Understand the relationship between customer service quality and on-time payment
- Be willing to translate this importance into face-to-face and written

communication with his customers
- Become familiar with the terminology of receivables – DSO, overdues, discrepancies, LRF
- Be able to address terms, discrepancy or other late-payment issues with customers without hesitation or discomfort
- Be ready to resolve customer discrepancies in a timely and professional manner (internal)
- Be able to work effectively with other internal functions who may need support in the resolution of customer discrepancies
- Be able to deal in a professional and positive way with customer objections to these changes
- When visiting the customer be ready to use observation, probing questions, and other tools to assess the health of the customer's business and recognise leading indicators of potential problems
- Build other relationships – including with competitor sales staff – so as to regularly elicit intelligence from them on who is doing well, not so well, paying late, etc.

Now it may be that your sales team are already comfortable with these tasks and are performing them routinely.

On the other hand, you may be finding that your sales team, perhaps already under pressure from declining sales or market disruption, are reluctant to engage with some of these changes.

Perhaps they do not see the point of them, think they are unhelpful, or, worse, interpret the requirement that they work in a new way as an implicit criticism of their past performance and competence.

How it works
Until you get the active understanding and support of your sales team, you may struggle to make a lasting impact on receivables.

But there is a right way and a wrong way to go about this – and it is vital that you do things in the right order so that you do not alarm or alienate your team.

This is the area of a receivables programme most likely to go wrong, because you are challenging the attitudes and behaviour of your internal "customer experts" and they may feel that their voice should be primary.

Be ready for alarmism
Often when organisations are starved of customer cash and leadership or finance presses for prompt collections, you may discover that sales (who to be fair are under other pressures) are unenthusiastic for fear of upsetting their customer or even "losing sales".

In fact, it is very common early in an improvement programme for sales leaders to caution the GM or CEO that if they are compelled to raise the issue of timely payment with customers, business is at risk and may be lost. This professional perspective is, we believe, mistaken, but must be taken seriously.

In addition, the false claim that letting customer credit grow will help to retain or grow sales is frequently promoted in order to deflect unwelcome pressure to change long-established attitudes and ways of working.

It is founded upon a series of misunderstandings which, left unchallenged, may prove terminal.

Before embarking on an exercise to bring customer payments into line, make sure you engage your sales team so they get a chance to express their concerns.

Start to explain the financial and service impacts of late payment, with examples.

Ideally, get them in a room with finance and others engaged in the process. Walk through the customer-to-cash process, capturing how it works, who does what, and where it goes wrong. Have those present consider solutions and rank them.

Get them to acknowledge that they are often forced to spend time with their (unhappy) customers dealing with areas of dissatisfaction, and that these discussions eat up valuable time and erode goodwill.

Stress throughout how important and valuable the commercial team is to the company. Position the exercise as a way to free up (valuable) sales from administration and bureaucracy so they can have more time to do what they do best.

If you have a large sales team (say 10-plus), poll them on how much time they actually spend on invoicing-related issues so as to demonstrate the benefits to them of fixing your invoicing and collections processes.

Late payment costs money – balance sheet basics

It is important to recognise that to a professional salesman raised on the need to build customer trust and grow sales, a new emphasis on receivables discipline may seem illogical and frustrating.

"We know they will pay," he may argue. "Why act as if we do not trust him and risk upsetting this profitable relationship?"

He may not understand that cash flow is a key element of financial performance, closely tracked by analysts, and that working capital has both a cost and a direct impact on profitability.

Step 1
Conceptual training: "Why the balance sheet matters". This is sometimes referred to as finance for non-finance managers.

Being first in line to get paid requires that – early on – you take steps to educate all non-financial staff, especially sales managers and salesmen and women, on how the balance sheet impacts actual performance, including cash flow and profitability.

If you take the time to build this conceptual foundation properly, all that follows will be much smoother. If you neglect or omit this, whether due to a sense of urgency or a crowded schedule, those without financial knowledge may continue to feel uncomfortable and perhaps "judged".

This discomfort will make the installation tricky and will make sustaining the changes even trickier.

Try to situate this conversation in real business examples that they will recognise – illustrations from their own accounts and some comparative scenarios work well.

Share real receivables performance data so that the multiple impacts of late payment can be clearly seen.

Consider sharing a benchmark of your DSO performance against selected competitors.

Be careful not to serve up irrelevant or misleading data – for example data on competitors who have different business models or a different market or customer mix. Only include these if you are equipped to explain differences and similarities in a way that supports your overall argument that "We need to do better".

Allow time for the subject to be properly explored and for all objections to be heard. If necessary, have more than one session.

Pay attention to who is supportive and who is less so. Be patient with those who are uncomfortable. They may remain hesitant until they see the new service processes working.

Look out for "luminaries" who quickly see the value of these changes and show a willingness to learn. Their example, once they start working the new processes successfully, often plays a key role in changing overall sentiment.

Later on, they may become trailblazers, willing to try new ways of talking to customers and to feed back their success (and challenges) to their peers.

Step 2
Engage sales in the development and wording of your credit policy.

The first step in getting a handle on receivables is to ensure you have clear credit terms and that these are formally accepted by the customer.

It is important to include the head of sales (and even sales managers) in your review of credit policy. This will allow their concerns to be aired and addressed and help them get familiar with a standard document that all of their customers will be required to sign.

You need to conduct the conceptual training in Step 1 first so that the business implications of a lack of formal credit terms are understood.

We urge you again not to hurry this – everything will go far more smoothly if your sales team understand *why* they need to ensure that their accounts acknowledge terms and pay in a timely fashion.

Ensure you have a thorough discussion where discomforts can be openly shared. Make it clear from the outset that it will be a sales responsibility to review payment terms with each account and ensure they are understood.

Step 3
Ensure sales are comfortable reviewing the written credit policy with their accounts. If this is new, pay close attention to it as the wrong message now will damage your ability to change things.

Once the policy is agreed internally, then the sales team will need to remind existing accounts of the details of the policy.

These details include a description of the new "proactive" service model that customers will receive and other changes which the customer must be made aware of *before* they are introduced.

Having this discussion, and backing it up with a letter, may prove challenging for some, so we recommend letting your luminaries run a pilot, reach out to selected accounts, and keep track of customer concerns or objections, so these can be workshopped with the rest of the team.

Step 4
Managing the sales meeting and using role-play to help build comfort with the new customer dialogue.

Once you have a clear policy and it has been communicated to customers, you may want to include in your regular sales meetings ongoing learning and role-play.

If you have a big team, you may want to organise a formal training session on the frustrations of dealing with customers who do not want to pay. Using scenarios and role-play, model typical customer reactions and suggest ways of dealing with objections in an amicable way.

Do make sure this is fun, and that your team does not feel threatened or judged. This may be unfamiliar territory to some, and a cause of discomfort or embarrassment. This is an opportunity to use a sales trainer who has experience dealing with customers in tricky collections situations and pairing her up with one or more luminaries in your own team.

Step 5
Refresh sales metrics to include late payments and discrepancy responsiveness.

Now you have a team who understand why receivables matter, have been involved in finalising the payment policy, and are starting to get practical experience in dealing with week-to-week discrepancy and collections challenges.

Now the time is right to review the bonus structure so that sales are paid at least in part on receivables outcomes.

This is a very tricky area and we stress that it is a mistake to hurry this change, lest you find yourself paying bonuses on outcomes over which your team do not feel that they have control.

At this early stage, we recommend you refer to this *only* as something that other companies do and ask them what they think.

Generating a transaction – invoice or invoice correction – is costly. If you doubt this, add up the total cost of your billing system, including labour, and divide it by the number of invoices you produce.

Typically, you will find that each transaction costs you at least US$100. I suggest you start to build a detailed picture for each account, starting with the biggest, of how much investigating and correcting discrepancies is costing, and, as things improve, how much is being saved.

Do

- Invest time in educating sales – and others – on balance sheet basics and the practical impacts of late payment.
- Poll sales and support staff on how much time they spend discussing accounts receivable with customers, and what issues customers typically report to them.
- Hold the line on terms given to new customers – and provide the right training.
- Closely manage a terms confirmation process with existing customers, bearing in mind the Pareto rule.
- Give your salesman the words to change the customer dialogue, from beginning to end, and practise until those words are second nature – include these FAQs into future sales training.
- Look for ambitious salesmen relatively free from bad habits who can be taught from scratch and become luminaries who influence the rest of the team.
- Develop data on customer errors being identified and resolved so the salesman can look informed and committed in front of the customer – some training will be needed to make this effective.
- Give account managers clear performance data overall and for their own accounts – friendly peer comparison does no harm!
- Once they understand why it matters, and have become comfortable with new topics and the language that goes with them, transition them to a bonus partially linked to customer payment performance (next chapter).
- Praise the salesmen who start to get it right.
- Celebrate tangible outcomes.

Do not
- Be frightened into silence by alarmism about losing customers.
- Try to do too much. As with all changes, trial them first with smaller accounts, learn and perfect.
- Make any changes to job descriptions, remuneration, reporting, etc., until your team have understood *at a conceptual level*:
  - Why receivables matter
  - How late payments impact profitability
  - How late payments eat up valuable sales time on admin and customer discussions
  - What the value of that sales time might be, if it could be spent on growing the business
  - What might happen if changes are not made to ensure timely customer payment (projected outcomes)
  - What they can do in their daily endeavours to support these changes

Make sales-variable pay work

From:
We will use new pay structures to force our people to become profit responsible.

To:
We will combine coaching and training to help our team take greater ownership of cross-functional outcomes, linked in due course to new variable pay.

In the last chapter we talked about what you should be measuring. Here we focus on how you should use variable pay linked to collections performance to ensure that your sales team pay attention both to how they *sell* and how they *collect*.

This book is specifically concerned with receivables.

Creating and maintaining the VRC always requires changes in the way that you measure and remunerate your team.

Since this is a sensitive and challenging exercise, it may make sense to consider a broader discussion about what you want to measure in future, both in general and in response to the uniquely challenging business conditions you find yourself in.

This is such a tricky issue that we are going to start with the Don'ts – because once your sales team are offside, it will be very hard to get them back onside.

Do not

- Introduce or even discuss variable pay linked to collections with your sales team until they have learned, through training, the importance of working capital to financial performance.
- Introduce variable pay linked to collections without using role-play-based training to get your sales team comfortable with having these conversations with their accounts, and dealing with common objections.
- Introduce variable pay linked to collections without ensuring that variable earnings are protected during the transition to the new scheme.

Do

- Poll your sales team on the AR issues they commonly encounter.
- Encourage your sales team to start recording customer feedback on receivables, *without* pressing them to act.
- Encourage your sales team to think about the time that they spend on receivables issues, in the office or face-to-face with customers.

Sales-variable pay

One of the most powerful tools in your ability to get paid on time is to incubate a sales culture with a financial interest in on-time, error-free customer payment.

But whenever you tinker with earnings you run the risk of causing fear, dismay and resentment.

If you have followed the steps laid out above you should have educated your sales team on why receivables matter, engaged them in policy development, and introduced them to your new service model, proactive calls and the critical importance of prompt issue resolution and systematic root cause elimination.

Now you are ready to start planning and introducing a sales incentive structure which specifically tracks and rewards:

- Timely payment
- Account DSO
- Reduced overdues
- Timely issue resolution

Timing and need for caution

Every company is different. A very small enterprise can explain and incorporate these changes fairly quickly and deal with concern or resistance more easily because the team is small.

As a general rule, the need for caution and diligence grows with the size and complexity of the enterprise.

So, for example, where you have large numbers of salesmen, geographies and divisions, you will want to treat changes to metrics and remuneration as a sensitive project that requires a proper process of change management. This is addressed in detail in Part 7: How to Make it Happen.

4.8 Balanced scorecard

By now, your leadership team, which has helped develop the credit policy and become actively engaged in discrepancy resolution, will understand how important it is for every function to get behind the VRC.

In Figure 4.18, we see an illustration of how different functions need to be engaged in building your VRC, and by implication, how measured.

Fig. 4.18 - TO MAKE CHANGES STICK, YOU WILL NEED TO PREPARE OTHER FUNCTIONS FOR NEW WAYS OF WORKING

	Leadership	Sales	Order Process	Manufacturing	Logistics	Billing	Collections	Finance	HR	After-Sales Service
Credit policy agreed	●	●	●	●	●		●	◐		●
Payment terms agreed, consistent	●	●	●			●	●	●		
Proactive collections			●		●	○	○			
Issue resolution SLA	○	●	●	●	●	●	●			●
Chronic negotiation	○	●	●	●						
Sales training	○	●							●	
Metrics & renumeration	●	●	●	◐	○	○	○	○	○	○
Job descriptions	●	●	●		●	●		●	●	○

Impact: ○ Low ◐ Med ● High   ILLUSTRATIVE

Every company is different but this should give you an idea of how to build a similar matrix for your own team.

In Figure 4.19 we show how different metrics – starting with DSO – can be applied cross-functionally to include:
- DSO
- Discrepancy resolution
- Root cause elimination
- Invoice accuracy
- Unbilled revenue

This is not a complete list and you may also want to include our working capital metrics, such as stock holding and service levels – these are outside the scope of this book.

Every function has a role to pay in ensuring you get paid on time. Engage key functions in training – see Fig 4.20 for ideas based upon a recent client.

Fig. 4.19 - EVERYONE HAS A ROLE TO PLAY IN SUPPORTING THE VIRTUOUS REVENUE CYCLE

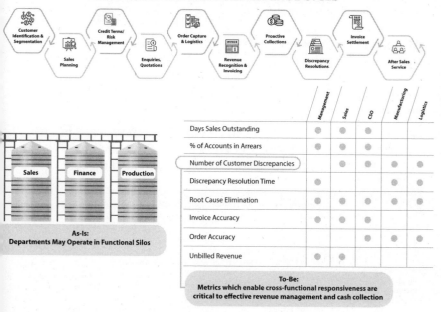

	Management	Sales	CSO	Manufacturing	Logistics
Days Sales Outstanding	●	●	●		
% of Accounts in Arrears	●	●	●		
Number of Customer Discrepancies		●	●	●	●
Discrepancy Resolution Time	●			●	●
Root Cause Elimination	●	●	●	●	●
Invoice Accuracy	●	●	●		
Order Accuracy			●	●	●
Unbilled Revenue	●	●			

As-Is:
Departments May Operate in Functional Silos

Sales   Finance   Production

To-Be:
Metrics which enable cross-functional responsiveness are critical to effective revenue management and cash collection

Fig. 4.20 - TRAINING FOR SALES AND OTHER FUNCTIONS SHOULD INCLUDE WORKING CAPITAL COMPONENTS

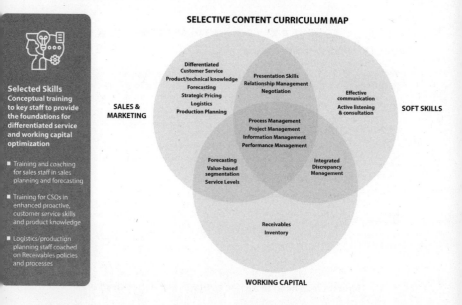

Selected Skills
Conceptual training to key staff to provide the foundations for differentiated service and working capital optimization

- Training and coaching for sales staff in sales planning and forecasting

- Training for CSOs in enhanced proactive, customer service skills and product knowledge

- Logistics/production planning staff coached on Receivables policies and processes

SELECTIVE CONTENT CURRICULUM MAP

SALES & MARKETING

SOFT SKILLS

WORKING CAPITAL

Differentiated Customer Service
Product/technical knowledge
Forecasting
Strategic Pricing
Logistics
Production Planning

Presentation Skills
Relationship Management
Negotiation

Effective communication
Active listening & consultation

Process Management
Project Management
Information Management
Performance Management

Forecasting
Value-based segmentation
Service Levels

Integrated Discrepancy Management

Receivables
Inventory

Ensure they are measured on receivables-related metrics.

In time, ensure their variable remuneration includes AR and discrepancy resolution measures

Understanding how roles will change

To achieve what is described here, you can now see that there will need to be changes in the way that your customer service team (CSO) – who may now be making the proactive calls and driving discrepancy resolution – and your sales team work and collaborate.

Fig. 4.21 - CUSTOMER SERVICE OFFICERS (CSOs) HAVE A KEY ROLE TO PLAY IN ENSURING EARLY CONTACT WITH CUSTOMERS AFTER INVOICING AND THE RESOLUTION OF DISCREPANCIES

KPI	DEFINITION	TRACKING FREQUENCY	WEIGHTING	RATIONALE
Total sales budget fulfilment	Actual total revenue/ total revenue budget	Monthly	30%	Maintaining existing accounts and winning next business a core Sales activity
Collections	Cash collected as % of Sales booked	Monthly	25%	Sales Reps/Managers need to share accountability for collections because their intervention plays key role - especially in communicating payment terms and resolving Sales related discrepancies
Customer retention	Unintended revenue loss of Tier 1 & 2 customers/previous year revenue	Six Months	15%	Maintaining existing accounts a core Sales activity
Contract management	% of contracts renewed on time and % of customers with signed agreement to payment terms	Quarterly	10%	Key driver of process quality - impacts annual price and margin increases, legal liabilities, confirmation of terms, and collections (e.g. through updating of PO numbers)
Discrepancy management	% of discrepancies resolved within target completion date	Quarterly	10%	- Need to ensure discrepancies resolved within target response date so cash can be collected without delay - Provide superior service to Tier 1 and 2 customers
Business specific	Other business-related objectives	TBD	10%	Business specific may have additional important business objectives - or can allocate weighting to other KPIs

Fig. 4.22 - SALES HAVE A KEY ROLE TO PLAY IN ENSURING CUSTOMER EXPECTATIONS ARE MET & OBSTACLES TO PAYMENT ARE REMOVED

KPI	DEFINITION	TRACKING FREQUENCY	WEIGHTING	RATIONALE
Total sales budget fulfilment	Actual total revenue/ total revenue budget	Monthly	30%	Maintaining existing accounts and winning next business a core Sales activity
Collections	Cash collected as % of Sales booked	Monthly	25%	Sales Reps/Managers need to share accountability for collections because their intervention plays key role - especially in communicating payment terms and resolving Sales related discrepancies
Customer retention	Unintended revenue loss of Tier 1 & 2 customers/previous year revenue	Six Months	15%	Maintaining existing accounts a core Sales activity
Contract management	% of contracts renewed on time and % of customers with signed agreement to payment terms	Quarterly	10%	Key driver of process quality - impacts annual price and margin increases, legal liabilities, confirmation of terms, and collections (e.g. through updating of PO numbers)
Discrepancy management	% of discrepancies resolved within target completion date	Quarterly	10%	- Need to ensure discrepancies resolved within target response date so cash can be collected without delay - Provide superior service to Tier 1 and 2 customers
Business specific	Other business-related objectives	TBD	10%	Business specific may have additional important business objectives - or can allocate weighting to other KPIs

**For meaningful performance management,
These metrics need to be tied to bonus / incentive structures**

Figures 4.21 and 4.22 describe how these roles might now look – every company is different so make your own – and should be read in conjunction with the audit templates at the end of the appendices in Part 9.

CSOs now have more responsibility for outcomes (remember we said how they were paid too little and lacked status?) and sales have to get to grips with DSO and responsiveness to discrepancies.

These tables suggest how variable remuneration might be allocated to reflect these changes – this is very sensitive so consider this carefully, but please do not ignore it because it signals your seriousness.

Part 5
Other opportunities

5.1 Reduce credit terms using BPDSO
5.2 Trade credit insurance
5.3 Leverage digital engagement

5.1 Reduce credit terms using BPDSO

We explained in Part 1 that outstanding receivables consist of:
- An element driven by the terms you offer – "terms-driven DSO"
- An element of overdues we call "process-driven DSO", which are overdue invoices that have become overdue because of something you did or failed to do

We did this to emphasise that late payments are generally a product of unmet customer expectations and can therefore be corrected by proactive contact, getting down to root causes, changing underlying processes, and eliminating the cause entirely.

Most companies we talk to have problems getting paid "to terms" – that is, they have a problem of overdues and want to reduce them.

Because overdues can be reduced more quickly than trading terms can be renegotiated, this book concentrates on helping you build a VRC, firm up on your pre-existing terms – eliminate any ambiguities – and use proactive service to encourage customers to pay to those terms.

What if you want to reduce your actual terms?
Once you are comfortable with your VRC and have seen your overdues come down as you have introduced the proactive service model and mobilised your sales team, you can carefully start to address the "terms" element of your DSO.

You have also been through a process of root cause elimination using LRF measures to stop costly discrepancies happening.

OTHER OPPORTUNITIES

127

Track your BPDSO

By calculating a weighted average BPDSO (Best Possible DSO) for current and previous quarters, you can see how your terms-driven DSO has altered over time.

Chances are that unless you have been giving it specific attention, it has been steadily creeping up.

Check out Figure 5.1 – which of these scenarios corresponds most closely to your situation?

Fig. 5.1 - UNDERSTAND YOUR DSO TREND - WHICH ONE CORRESPONDS MOST CLOSELY TO YOUR SITUATION?

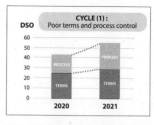
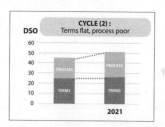
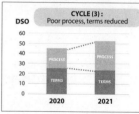
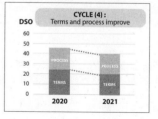

It is most likely to be Cycle 1 – you have seen both process and terms-driven DSO creep up over time.

What you want to do is to move to Cycle 4 – you have started to reduce process-driven DSO using the VRC, now you want to start looking at opportunities to ensure your terms are kept under control.

1. Prevent your BPDSO growing further
2. Selectively reduce your BPDSO as and when possible
3. Ensure you are now on Cycle 4

Opportunity model

To accomplish this you will need to model your BPDSO. Using data you should have gathered earlier in Part 2, you can put your customers on a matrix. See Figure 5.2 for the suggested matrix.

Fig. 5.2 - IS YOUR INVESTMENT IN CUSTOMER WORKING CAPITAL CONSISTENT WITH THE VALUE OF THE CUSTOMER?

(1) Build The Matrix

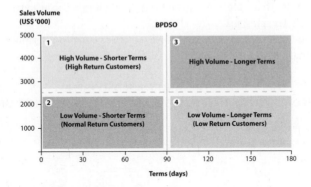

Using this matrix, you can compare the economic contribution of each customer (or sales volume if you lack contribution data) with their agreed and actual payment terms.

To keep this simple, you may want to remember the Pareto principle and start with your top 20% biggest customers.

Fig. 5.3 - IS YOUR INVESTMENT IN CUSTOMER WORKING CAPITAL CONSISTENT WITH THE VALUE OF THE CUSTOMER?

(2) Populate Matrix with Actual Customers, Starting with the Top 20%

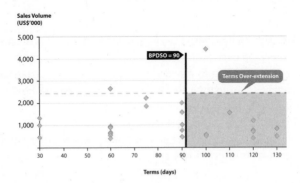

The vertical line in the middle represents the theoretical BPDSO of this group of customers based upon their agreed terms (remember this is terms, not actual DSOs).

Any customer whose payment terms sit on the right-hand side of this line is causing your BPDSO to rise, and on the left, to fall.

You should quickly see that in Quadrant 4 there are some outliers who generate little value but have a negative (upward) impact on BPDSO.

You will also see some high contributors in Quadrant 3.

Migration strategy

Fig. 5.4 - IS YOUR INVESTMENT IN CUSTOMER WORKING CAPITAL CONSISTENT WITH THE VALUE OF THE CUSTOMER?

(3) Develop Migration Plans

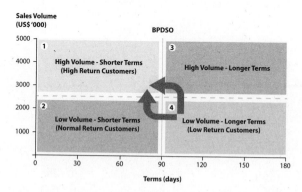

For customers in Quadrants 3 and 4, check their discrepancy history and see how you have performed in eliminating root cause process errors and improving their overall service levels.

How strong is your relationship?

Can you think of other services or attributes that you could offer them to reduce their costs or improve their efficiency?

Remember, if you have eliminated discrepancies by addressing root causes, this means you have *already* delivered lower transaction costs for both you and your customer. Do the math.

Quadrant 4

Smaller customers who deliver little value but who take a long time to pay should be politely encouraged to commit to shorter payment terms. Every day by which you can shorten their terms will move the BPDSO line to the left. In many cases, you can be firm.

Quadrant 3

Bigger customers who deliver value but take a long time to pay are the ones to give your utmost attention to.

Bigger companies typically have deeper pockets and more options.

Changing their terms, even by a little, will have a disproportionate impact on your BPDSO.

Together with your sales account manager, work through some ideas for reducing their agreed terms.

Fig. 5.5 - VICIOUS TO VIRTUOUS

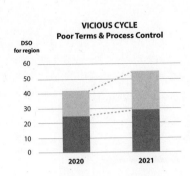
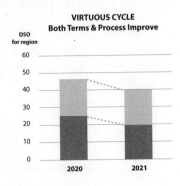

You are aiming to control both the terms mix you offer customers, as measured by BPDSO, and the level of overdues in your DSO, which you do by building a VRC with proactive customer contact.

Steps
1. Create a model, based on the template we show above.
2. Share it with the sales team, and invest time in ensuring they understand it.
3. Share root cause elimination data by account so as to establish where your VRC has helped cut customer costs.
4. Encourage your sales colleagues to identify opportunities to move selected customers to the left, leveraging the cordial relations generated by the now established VRC.
5. Use the opportunity of the review period included in your signed credit policy to table some options to the customer.
6. One or two victories by a sales luminary will in our experience really bring this to life.
7. Make this process a routine part of your internal dialogues so that your BPDSO starts to decline quarter by quarter.

Do
- Wait until your new service model is firmly in place and you have evidence of reduced late payments before looking at this.

- Accumulate good data on customers where discrepancy rates have come down due to your great teamwork.
- Get your team used to solid progress on root cause elimination, in each case stressing positive LRF impacts.
- Encourage your team to come up with new and innovative ways to help your customers and add value.
- Be firm about reducing terms or increasing prices for small customers who deliver little profit but pay late and are more costly to serve.
- Make this part of your regular sales meetings, and reward success.

Do not
- Start your VRC programme by trying to renegotiate terms. With late payments still an issue and without data on root causes, you run the risk of damaging customer relations.
- Socialise this part of the programme to your team until real progress on overdues and service quality is visible to all.
- Try and yank customer payment terms back to some externally sourced benchmark – base your discussions on the current reality.

5.2 Trade credit insurance

Trade Credit Insurance is a product that allows a seller to insure receivables against customer default. The product covers the relationship between a supplier and a buyer where the supplier trades products and services on open credit terms.

Credit insurance has been around for 130 years and the top global insurers are AIG, Euler Hermes, Zurich Insurance Group, COFACE and Atradius.

This chapter is based on interviews with industry insiders, including Euler Hermes and others.

How it works
Insurers offer the creditor who takes out trade credit insurance three elements:

1. Tracking credit-worthiness
Insurers monitor and assess the customer portfolio (buyers). We monitor the credit-worthiness or the probability of default of these buyers, over 12 months, and give advice to the creditor about the strength of his buyer portfolio.

So before onboarding the client, we assess their portfolio, and then throughout the policy year we monitor these buyers and give advice real-time.

We track and report any deterioration or improvement in the buyer portfolio for individual buyers. If a company, all of a sudden, is in trouble and stops paying other suppliers, whom we also insure, we are able to give a warning to that specific policyholder saying this company is in trouble.

Our aim is to use this intelligence to help our client to de-risk. We need to help him reduce his exposure over time – and our early warning system, which gets better as we scale up, gives him early access to critical intelligence.

2. Collection services

Our second service is collections. If a default occurs and it's not from an insolvency – meaning that the debtor is still continuing to operate but has a cash flow problem and cannot pay his debt to his creditors – we step in and negotiate on behalf of the supplier, with the buyer, a satisfactory repayment plan.

Of course we make sure that we bring several suppliers whom we insure to the table and we say, in effect, "We have a big book, you'd better start paying our suppliers because we are stepping in on their behalf, and we urge you to prioritise our policyholders."

Otherwise, we may have to stop insuring several of your suppliers. If that happens – and we would rather strike a deal – it will be painful because you will either no longer get the goods that you need for manufacturing, or you may have to pay cash on delivery. This may affect your cash flow and bring you even deeper downwards.

3. Indemnification

We are insurers, so if there is really something going wrong and if the debtor with a protected default cannot pay even after we have tried to collect, after a certain time we would pay out.

Of course, if there is an insolvency or a court judgment, we pay the creditor immediately without any waiting period.

In credit insurance, it is important that we like our policyholders to "have skin in the game", so normally we will only indemnify 90% of the total credit limit, leaving a 10% exposure with the policyholder.

It is therefore a partnership where the insured party has a clear interest in working with us to seek a settlement with the debtor.

Value proposition to SMEs

Insurers can deliver value in a number of ways. SMEs often lack the manpower internally to employ a big credit management department of their own.

By entering into a contract with an insurer, they effectively outsource their credit management to us. And in return we like to have policyholders who work hand-in-hand with us, giving early updates if they hear anything about buyer problems.

In Singapore, for example, the government encourages SMEs to take up trade credit insurance. Under the TCIS (Trade Credit Insurance Scheme), the government sponsors 50% of the premium in order to entice SMEs to enter into trade credit.

The Singapore government realises this is a very important product in mature markets for the trading ecosystem. It helps national suppliers of goods and services to be competitive.

SMEs who trade with MNCs

Many SMEs enter into contracts with much bigger companies and the commercial terms are quite one-sided in favour of the larger company. The relationship is asymmetrical.

So having the peace of mind that an insurance company can bring is very important.

Our research shows that if a company goes insolvent, the root cause is often that one of their main buyers has defaulted.

This dynamic is especially prevalent in the SME segment, because they rely disproportionately on one big buyer. Should that relationship collapse, then the whole cash flow of that company gets into trouble.

COVID and other impacts

Euler Hermes' economic research team reports that 2020 showed lower insolvency numbers than 2019 in many countries. Very counter-intuitive. But the reason is that during COVID's onset, the government started subsidy schemes, and even took legal steps. Business courts were closed. You couldn't get a judgment on insolvency and they even delayed the insolvency process in some countries.

Some European governments, which have entered into an almost symbiotic partnership with trade credit insurers, in order to give government support, asked credit insurers not to reduce capacity, and to keep covering suppliers in the German or UK or French market as before.

I think the hope was that by getting through the crisis you could get the company to restart, maybe within 12 months or so.

But as it turned out, the economy has stayed depressed as the pandemic drags on. The longer the recovery takes, the less likely this scenario becomes.

US China policy

Trump's policy forced trade credit insurers and their policyholders to think deeply about their China supply chains.

Because of this, even before COVID, insurers had already encouraged policyholders to de-risk, to look at certain China SOEs and others where we had to reduce exposures for our policyholders. So we had already mitigated quite a lot of things pre-COVID.

Nobody could see COVID coming but through this trade war supply chain management, and the exposures deriving from it, a lot of work was done by trade credit insurers.

The risk mitigation measures developed by corporates because of the trade war suddenly became very useful when COVID happened.

How do I get trade credit insurance?

Companies seeking insurance fill in a questionnaire. They list buyer relationships with names, IDs (in Singapore ACRA details), whatever, as detailed as possible.

They also give an overview of past bad debts or write-offs. If they are able, they submit an aging report – how many days their invoices are overdue.

All this information gets put by the insurer into an underwriting model, which assesses the buyers listed based on credit-worthiness. They are then graded using the insurer's own model and a credit limit is determined based on the customer mix.

Encouraging clients to reduce exposure

We are happy that you sell on an open credit terms, but we may cover 100%, or we may cover 80% depending on what we know.

We go through your portfolio and give you the customer grades, from 1 to 10. 1 is the best credit rating whilst 10 is basically defaulted!

We would not normally insure a 10, 9, or 8; and for a 7, cover would be very limited. Sometimes we also sit down with you and say, "What is your credit management manual? Please show us how you are collecting how you incentivise your salespeople to be involved in the collection process. "

Pricing

The insurer puts all this into their pricing tool, which also then determines the commercial terms. The policy itself is then drafted, including credit limits and fees.

Your customer list changes

The insurer may onboard a set of 20 buyers with a policy for 12 months.

If after, say, three months your sales team finds a new customer, the new buyer is added to the portfolio.

The insurer reverts with a yes/no: this customer credit limit is acceptable, or "We need to look at this", or "We don't know that buyer" – which should not happen that often, but we ask "Can you facilitate that we call them up so we can talk to them about management experience and all of their financial KPIs (if there are no open financial statements published)?"

Buyer visits or buyer calls nowadays are very important and that's why insurers have a big team in this area to really go into the details.

In cases where a client brings on a new customer, the insurer makes a premium adjustment.

Rates

Rates are calculated on annual turnover and revised at the end of the policy year. If the 20 customers at the beginning of the policy period generate $100m, the insurer gives a rate of, say, 0.15% of your turnover.

This can be higher depending on the quality of your customer portfolio. Under COVID, rates are of course going up, since credit risk is increasing.

It might be 0.25% or 0.35% depending on where you are, where you're selling, or if you want to have special conditions in the policy. But let's say for safety sake 0.3% on your turnover.

How to claim

There are different situations. You have your invoice which is, let's say, due in 90 days. After that due date, you have a so-called MEP – maximum extension period – which is normally 30 days. You can keep on trading with that company because sometimes invoices are not paid because of the admins.

So you continue to supply if you negotiate this in your policy terms.

Of course, at the moment, under COVID, we try to restrict MEPs. They used to be sometimes 60 days or longer. Nowadays we really bring it down to 30 days or don't offer MEP at all.

And then, after the MEP, if they're not paid, then the buyer enters into the so-called state of default. We would then ask you for your notification, and go into collection activities.

Partnering with bank lenders/factors

When approaching a bank for a loan on accounts receivable, the bank will typically look at the portfolio and say "Here are my receivables from these 10 countries, 10 companies. And would you like to buy them?"

And of course the bank would say yes, and then they look at the buyer portfolio – if they're comfortable they would say yes. And they would say, I give you a discount because you get the money. Earlier, I buy it at 95% of the value, or 92% depending on my risk and we charge the bank, the bank becomes the policyholder for that specific debt and they pass on the cost.

Companies who have their receivables insured can take their policy to the bank and say, "I'm insured by Euler Hermes – would you like to buy our receivables so we get the cash in advance?"

With Euler Hermes' double-A rating, the banks know the client will be indemnified against a default so they may give a more preferential term to the supplier for their receivables.

In effect, the bank becomes a beneficiary in the policy. If a client enters into a factoring arrangement, the bank becomes a beneficiary in the policy between us and the policyholder.

5.3 Leverage remote working and digital engagement

At the time of writing, remote working is widespread in much of the business world. Forced into working from home, many are getting used to conducting business via Zoom and other apps. Some 74% of companies plan to permanently shift to more remote work after COVID.

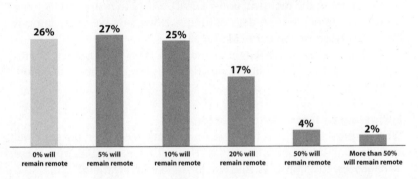

Fig. 5.6 - 74% OF COMPANIES PLAN TO PERMANENTLY SHIFT TO MORE REMOTE WORK POST COVID-19

Intimacy lies at the heart of the VRC. By looking your customer in the eye and resolving any unmet expectation civilly, promptly and reliably, you build respect and trust.

We have especially stressed the importance of maintaining close contact with key customers.

Consider initiating and maintaining Zoom contact with selected customers so you can increase intimacy and grow your relationship.

This is a good time to change how you operate, as many of your customers will be going through the same learning curve that you have and will have changed their attitudes to digital communication.

Resistance

There may be many different people in your organisation who normally interact with customers face-to-face or by phone.

Ask yourself which activities now performed in person or by phone could be done digitally, and what the benefits might be.

Of those people who might be involved in digital communication, how strong are their skills and will they need coaching and encouragement?

Make the case for change and help ready them for digital communication – these are vital skills for the future world of business.

Selected activities

Remember that digital platforms can be used to see and talk to an important customer and enable these parts of the VRC:
- Build a new relationship
- Onboard a customer unavailable to meet in person
- Share documents and data, including credit policy
- Address gaps, concerns and FAQs

Discrepancy resolution, account review

In the past, the tendency for different customer conversations to be inconsistent or protracted harmed relationships and delayed payment.

You can now engage the customer, your account manager, the resolver (if different) and the co-ordinator in one call.

This has the potential to improve clarity and alignment and reduce cycle times for resolution and payment.

In summary

By going digital you can:
- Track progress via shared reports
- Conduct joint training and communication
- Establish intimacy with key customer staff (start when you are onboarding them)

- Respond more quickly to discrepancies
- Engage internal Resolvers in discussions with the customer
- Differentiate yourself from other, clunkier suppliers

It is about being first in line to get paid. If you go out of your way to be more visible to your customer, you are more likely to be treated better. Once they see the value in digital face-to-face, customers may often elect to continue even after normal working returns.

Do not miss this opportunity.

Do

- Take advantage of changed perceptions about virtual communication to change your customer's perception of you.
- Build digital skills in your own team – everyone who has customer contact should be readied for digital.
- Consider which parts of customer contact you can do via digital channels.
- Identify customers who are themselves learning to work digitally and might be more open.
- Be ready to explain to customers what the value to them might be.
- Selectively trial digital contact, make it work for you and make it a standard option for the future.
- Have cross-functional account calls internally and with your customer to demonstrate your team approach and resolve discrepancies collaboratively.
- Consider how you can improve new customer onboarding, set-up and policy agreement.
- Consider how to conduct proactive and service calls with top customers.
- Keep it going post-COVID where you can.

Do not

- Be afraid to innovate – the world has changed.
- Be put off by colleagues who are uncomfortable with digital.
- Simply wait for things to go back to normal post-COVID.
- Let resistance within your team derail this.

Part 6
Your start-up advantage

6.1 Why do start-ups fail?

Perhaps you are here because you are contemplating a start-up, or perhaps you are already starting up?

You will already know, probably, that most start-ups fail. But the thing is, they do not fail due to a lack of creative ideas or even due to a lack of customers.

When they fail, it is mostly because they run out of cash. This is because rapid growth, gratifying though it is, often requires increasing amounts of working capital if it is to be sustained.

Generally in business you have to make the product or deliver the good or service before you can ask to be paid. If you are making lots more product or if you are investing more and more resources in delivering products or services and if you are doing all that before you get paid – then you risk running out of the cash you need to run the business.

What may then happen
Often a good business idea which takes off quickly needs more cash to be invested as working capital to support growing demand.

If the cash cannot be found and current liabilities – like rent, salaries or supplier payments – cannot be met, then insolvency looms.

You may fold, or in some heart-breaking cases you may find yourself handing over a big chunk of your business to an investor with the ready cash to sustain you. This is a horrible pill to swallow when the ideas and the energy are all your own.

Fortunately you are here reading this book, and will find in these pages the solutions you need to:

- Be clear to your team about the importance of working capital discipline

– build receivables metrics into your team measurement right from the start
- Model your working capital needs effectively from the outset and plan your cashflow using the template we provide
- From the outset, include firm payment discussions in your customer interactions (as well as your suppliers')
- Build a Virtuous Revenue Cycle into your operating model from day one so as to maximise cash inflow
- Understand potential funding needs from the beginning and be in a position to source what additional lending or investment you may need ahead of time
- Track changing working capital needs and be ready for them when they occur

It is no exaggeration to say that by starting off on the right foot – with this book – you have made it very unlikely that you will be one of those who run out of cash.

6.2 The right foot

When you are small and the team is busy figuring out new stuff and finding your market, it may seem that the last thing you need is to worry about payment terms, invoicing and other "administrative" tasks.

Building a healthy operating model where the cash flows in smoothly will be far easier if you do it from the outset than if you neglect it, run into liquidity issues and have to grapple with difficulties reactively.

Actually that is the key message of this book. But unlike established enterprises who have to fundamentally change their customer engagement model to get cash flow under control when it goes wrong, all the start-up business has to do is to get a few simple things right from the beginning:

- Clear service and payment policy for all customers from the beginning – no exceptions – as part of your professional culture
- Importance of policy understood and supported by the whole team – no exceptions
- Any team member with customer interaction to be comfortable with articulating this aspect of your culture, and challenging objections whenever they present themselves
- Investment in a high-touch service model for the top 20% from the outset – sounds grand but might be one person

- Firm policy on non-compliant customers where there is no discrepancy at issue – watch the rollover
- Model your cash needs, revisit the model, anticipate and plan for potential gaps
- Stay on top of discrepancies and eliminate them quickly
- Make life binary and communicate the same positive message about cash and service that you do about your product!
- Consider digital enablement of your service model

6.3 SME checklist

So that you can make sure all these important pieces are in place, we have developed an SME checklist with references to templates included in the appendices.

Fig. 6.2 - SME CHECKLIST

Type	Item	How Measured
Communication	Credit Policy	Completed template
	Internal announcement	Completed template
	Customer terms letter	Completed template
Service toolkit	Pareto first 10%	Completed template
	Pareto first 20%	Completed template
	Collections intensity matrix	Completed template
	Automated collections	Completed template
	Proactive call script (adapted)	Completed template
	Call tracking sheet	Completed template
	Discrepancy Resolution framework	Completed template
Mobilise commercial team	Sales collections target-selling	Completed template
The perfect invoice	Discrepancy incidence by type	Completed template
	Discrepancy resolution time scale	Completed template
	Discrepancy resolution by salesman	Completed template
	Discrepancy resolution top accounts	Completed template
Measure and win	Rollover reduction	Completed template
	Chronic reduction	Completed template
	DSO reduction overall	Completed template
	DSO reduction top accounts	Completed template
	DSO reduction by salesman	Completed template
	BPDSO quarterly trend	Completed template
	Bad debt trend	Completed template
	LRF and trends	Completed template

Part 7
How to make it happen

From:
We need to get this done so we can't waste time worrying about details, causes or opinions.

To:
We will take the time needed to build internal understanding and consensus so that we can make real changes that will last.

Accelerated approach

We realise that some who arrive at this page will be under pressure to execute rapid high-impact actions to reduce late payments and get more cash in, quickly. You are in a hurry.

To help those of you under pressure, we have provided in Fig 6.1 a simple checklist of what needs to be done and in what order, intended for small SMEs who have few staff and simple operations.

If you seek lasting (rather than temporary) change, and especially if you have more than 50 staff in more than one geography, we strongly encourage you to follow the steps in this book, in the order in which they are laid out.

7.1 Value discovery – Why do it at all?

Many companies enjoy brief – but not sustained – success when they start emphasising the importance of cash flow improvement and DSO reduction.

This is often because they skip the "value discovery" required to build a solid case for change within the organisation (starting with the leadership team). Or because they fail to take the time, having built a case for change, to properly test and install the changes required to change service culture in the fundamental way required.

Do not be alarmed. We are not trying to over-complicate things, but just suggesting a logical sequence of actions based on *agreed business value* that will maximise your chances of success.

Sadly, we know companies that have tried repeatedly to make lasting changes to receivables performance. They have instead achieved short periods of improvement followed by a return to their prior situation, though often with understandable frustration and a further reinforcement of the commonly held myths that lay the blame elsewhere.

What is value discovery?

Value discovery is the process of uncovering the total business benefits of moving to a VRC in your company.

The objective is, as we have said, to quickly build a very compelling case for change, based on solid evidence of commercial opportunity.

Even if you are making these changes because you are reacting to a shortage of cash, it is important that the broader impacts of the VRC – overwhelmingly positive – are factored into your programme.

This is so that you can:

- Clearly show the total financial benefits of moving to the VRC
- Share those benefits with your entire leadership team to strengthen the case for change so it cannot easily be challenged
- Show how different functions impact receivables outcomes
- Show that lasting change is only possible if those functions engage in the process and commit to long-term change
- Link specific parts of your change process to specific business outcomes
- Develop a set of success measures which include financial and non-financial metrics, and can be quickly adopted (we mentioned some of these at the end of Part 4)

Guiding principles

- Value is total business impact (i.e. not just cash flow or DSO).
- Without fixing the causes, changes will not last.
- Everyone is involved.
- Total honesty is essential on gaps and causes.

7.2 The elements of value discovery

The elements of value discovery include, broadly, collecting relevant data on the current and *projected* business situation and defining the full business value of following a VRC programme.

Fig. 7.1 - THE KEY STEPS

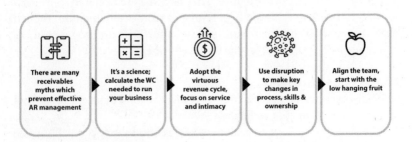

By now we have gone over the key steps in some detail, but Figure 7.1 reminds us that, contrary to widespread belief, the ability to control AR levels and DSO is not an arcane science but a result of clear policy and coordinated action.

Using the tools described in this book you should be able to calculate what your working capital needs are based upon mathematical projections of your customer and terms mix and the quality of your processes.

Fig. 7.2 - THE OBSTACLES

You need to be ready to counter misconceptions – and deliberate resistance – by understanding your prevailing culture and taking time to address concerns. We addressed many of these concerns earlier in the book but Figure 7.2 reminds us what they are likely to include.

Internal resistance is your biggest challenge and you need to be ready.

Fig. 7.3 - FIRST PROCESS, THEN TERMS

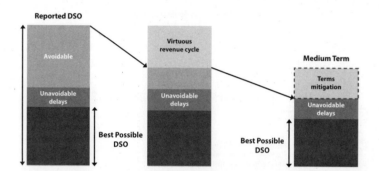

1. First you reduce overdues by eliminating avoidable delays. You do this by clarifying your credit policy and increasing the nature and timing of customer interactions, linked to systematic discrepancy resolution.
2. In due course, with LRF root-cause evidence assembled, you can gradually attempt to reduce your customer terms mix and freeze, then reduce, your BPDSO.

Fig. 7.4 - CURRENT TREND (DO NOTHING) vs VRC PROGRAMME

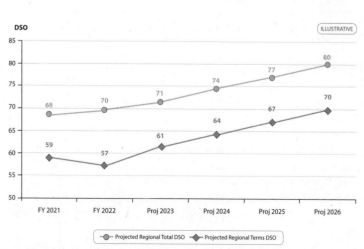

To get internal attention, we strongly advocate projecting your future DSO – and receivables $ – based on your current trends, if you were to simply do nothing.

To do this you will need to use regression analysis, going back over your DSO performance by quarter for at least a year, as well as your BPDSO.

Create a chart like Figure 7.4 which takes that data and says "Here's where we will be in a year" if we do nothing.

Then take the projected DSO for the next few years and multiply it by your projected sales increase. This has the effect of showing a very large growth in your nominal receivables working capital.

By assembling the data below and assessing the impact of a VRC programme, you can define the benefits of improving process and terms – see Fig 7.5 for the actual benefits of a recent (disguised) client programme.

Fig. 7.5 - ACT ON PROCESS, THEN TERMS

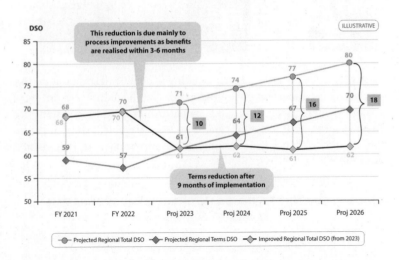

By acting on process (VRC installation), then on terms (using LRF data), we can project a dramatic difference in DSO within 4–6 months. In this compelling instance, a deteriorating trend is checked, reversed, and sustained.

1. Data analysis

In summary, when evaluating current AR performance, it is useful to look at what would happen to the business if you were to carry on with "business as usual".

For example, if overdues show a worsening trend, what happens when you project this trend forward, adjusting for sales growth and increasing DSO?

- What is the underlying trend in revenue and overdues? (Use quarterly data points)
- How do your overdues break down between rollover and chronic (rollover: 0–30; chronic: 31+)?
- What percentage of current invoices rolls over into overdue every month?
- What percentage of customer invoices contain errors?
- Based upon a few selected examples, how long can it take to resolve errors? (Best, worse, average)
- What are the main billing errors reported by customers, and how much revenue does each type of error hold up?
- What is the value of overdue receivables with the top 20% of your customers?
- What might be the impact on each of these variables by following the steps laid out in Parts 4 and 5?

2. Selective time use analysis

- How much sales time is spent on pursuing receivables and resolving billing errors? (See Figure 1.6 in Part 1 for how this is measured, and how it is underestimated!)
- Once things settle down and the VRC is in place, how much additional sales time will be freed and what would be the impact of this additional time on new business acquisition?
- How much admin time is spent chasing receivables and resolving billing errors? This is another efficiency gain.

3. Business case for change (Summary)

- What will happen if you do nothing (as opposed to launching an improvement programme)?
- What would be the benefits of undertaking an AR improvement programme?
  - More cash available (programme versus doing nothing)
  - Reduced borrowing (programme versus doing nothing)
  - OPEX savings from fewer invoice errors
  - Happier customers (impact on retention)
  - More sales time available to sell (convert additional time into sales)

Remember, time invested in doing a proper investigation will help you build a solid case for change, get the team behind you, and increase the speed and effectiveness of the changes you then make. Resist the urge to park all this and rush into things.

7.3 Building support – Why does change fail?

When planning a move to the VRC, it is useful to understand that changes of this kind often fail, and the reasons are generally well known as a result of lots of analysis over the years.

Data shows that, for example, around 80% of business change programmes fall short of their objectives.

A change programme is one that to be successful will require a large percentage of your people to change working practices they have become used to and to think in a new way and work differently.

Since adopting the VRC in order to be first in line to get paid requires that leadership, finance, sales, logistics, and others adopt new ways of working, it is a significant undertaking.

Fig. 7.6 - WE HAVE TRACKED MORE THAN 200 VRC IMPLEMENTATION INITIATIVES TO UNDERSTAND WHY THEY FAIL AND WHAT CAN BE DONE ABOUT IT

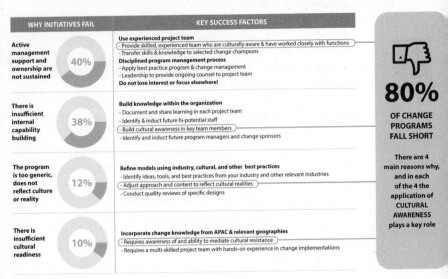

It is cultural resistance and poor communication that prevents success, mostly, and the lack of a clear business case and justification has a key role to play.

In Figure 7.6 we list what we have learned from carrying out VRC programmes around the world, with the intention of stressing the need to be sensitive to cultural differences. Change is often perceived as a threat, and without engaging, listening, communicating, you may find that some operations or geographies move much more slowly than others.

Take time to explore these risks and mitigate them with fact-based communication.

Internal, not external

It cannot be stressed enough that the most important factor in changing your AR outcomes will be the *internal* changes you make to the way your team think, behave towards each other and to customers, and which later on will be tracked, measured and paid.

You need to shed any notion that the main causes of late payment are external and therefore beyond your control or the control of your team.

It is very likely that this mistaken belief will confront you as you begin and resurface regularly as you go about making changes.

For SMEs

For an SME in one geography, it may be comparatively simple to launch and track these changes. You see your team regularly, so you can directly address the problem and quickly assess resistance or concern.

In our case studies, for three very different companies, although external advice on what to change was taken, the actual process of change depended heavily on top-down leadership and ownership.

Use the checklist in Part 6.

For larger companies

For a company with multiple personnel and multiple geographies, however, even an SME, challenges may arise.

An understanding of how people react to change and how to support them through it may be helpful and we offer a useful framework here: AUBC – awareness, understanding, buy-in, commitment.

The key to using this methodology lies in identifying different groups in your company, and then using workshops, online surveys and multiple levels of communication to help each group through the process of change.

Before you launch any kind of communication and evaluation of change readiness, you will want to understand the value of making these changes and the change priorities – what needs to be fixed and in what order.

7.4 Sequencing the changes

If you are a large entity and have a lot going on, it makes sense to break down the elements of the VRC programme into sub-initiatives and prioritising them on a simple matrix. The difficulty y-axis should be based on an honest assessment of available resources and resistance.

Fig. 7.7 - SEQUENCING THE CHANGES
- when considering which elements of your VRC to do first, it may help to use an initiative prioritization matrix

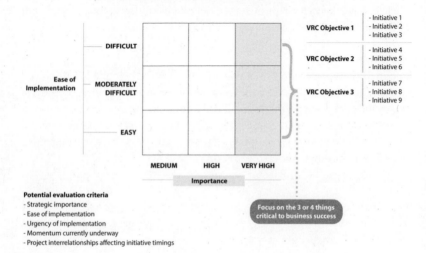

This will give you priority actions as well as a sense of where your risks lie and how you can actively mitigate them.

Do use this approach to test different scenarios with your leadership so that they understand the main activities and their role.

There are two things to consider when making major changes to the way your team thinks and works.

Managing change

The first, often neglected, is the need to build a strong case for change, so that everyone concerned sees why changes are needed, and to maintain a continuous programme of communication and coaching throughout the changes. Properly managed, this will prevent pushback and accelerate the adoption of the new behaviours and processes.

Sequencing the changes
There is a right way to do things. The VRC includes a number of building blocks which are essential to success but need to be laid out in the right order.

Main steps
- Why do we need to change?
- What needs to change?
- Who will be affected?
- What does the change look like?
- Who will pilot it first?
- How will we measure success?

By planning the right sequence using these building blocks you can plan the changes over time (see Figure 7.8):

Fig. 7.8 - YOUR VRC PROGRAM MAY LOOK SOMETHING LIKE THIS - BUT MAKE IT YOUR OWN!

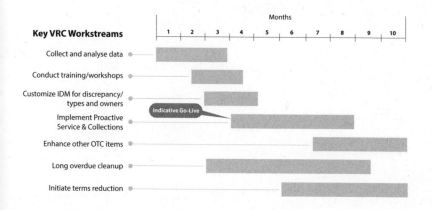

You will need to think about a project structure – especially if your organisation is large and complex. Even in a small SME, each of these elements needs attention (see Figure 7.9).

Figure 7.10 summarises the same programme but from a benefit flow timing perspective. Your DSO reduces at different rates depending on where you are in the VRC sequence. These timings are surprisingly constant, across almost all VRC programmes. It is worth sharing and discussing them.

Fig. 7.9 - IN MOST ORGANISATIONS OF ANY SIZE, IT IS LIKELY THAT IMPLEMENTING THE VRC WILL BREAK DOWN INTO THESE WORK STREAMS

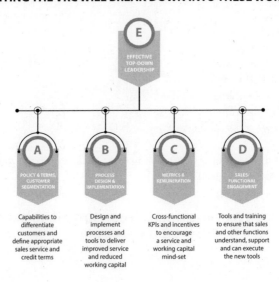

Fig. 7.10 - VRC PROGRAMME: IMPACT OVER TIME

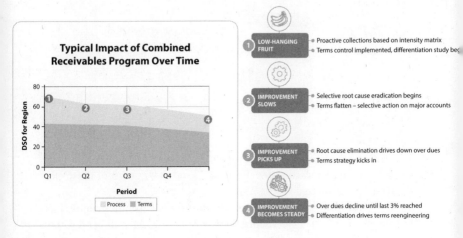

Fig. 7.11 - IT IS ALL ABOUT VALUE

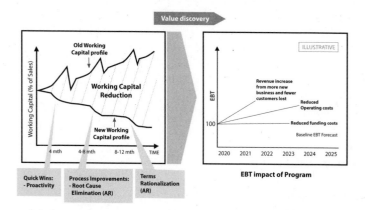

By following the steps described here, you should have been able to calculate an "old working capital profile" where you do nothing and a "new working capital profile" where you implement the VRC.

These changes can then be factored into a Programme Impact calculation which shows the direct impact on financial results over time.

7.5 Outcome-based training

Most classroom learning degrades to nothing within two months unless it is brought into a real business context and applied directly to customer situations and tracked post-classroom.

There is a great deal of compelling data on this. Despite it, training tends to be classroom-based (or digital classroom) and is rarely applied with any consistency to the real work environment.

We therefore strongly advocate the following steps in delivering training to your team.

1. Understanding the message
Start with conceptual balance-sheet training – sometimes called "finance for non-financial managers".

Make the conceptual case for the Virtuous Revenue Cycle using the elements of value discovery laid out above.

- What failure at each step is costing
- Why leadership and sales need to get involved
- What the business outcome of installing the VRC would be
- How functional roles would change

2. Applying the message

In a second (practical) session, have sales and leadership bring specific customer situations (active case studies) to the training.

- Role-play the challenges
- Align them with the VRC steps
- Agree specific actions for each account owner
- Identify and mobilise luminaries
- Commit to a timeline

3. Carrying the message

In a series of follow-up sessions, report on the outcomes achieved and obstacles encountered.

- Role-play both positive and negative outcomes
- Capture solutions in an FAQ document
- Reinforce the session regularly as part of routine sales and leadership meetings
- Capture the training, digitise it, make it available to recruits and the newly promoted

Follow-up and audit can be helped by using templates such as the ones included in the appendices.

Remember, the point about audit (feel free to call it something else) is that the expectations should be shared from early in the programme. You want people to pass with flying colours, not fall behind and fail!

Part 8
Postscript

Fig. 8.1 - RECEIVABLES ROLLER COASTER

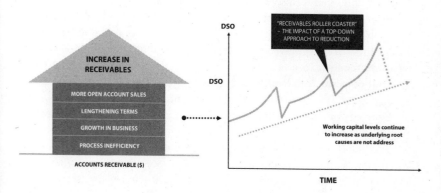

8.1 It's a journey

You cannot "fix" working capital and move on. In commerce, customers and markets evolve, disruptions occur and situations change.

In the healthiest of businesses things, alter constantly. Winners are fast on their feet and ready to change course at short notice.

It is always possible to impact customer payments and DSO by aggressive action after the event but this is *not* a strategy for business success as it risks alienating customers. It is a very short-term approach.

The VRC, correctly understood and employed, ensures you are closer to your customers than your competitors are and in a better position to identify potential issues (and opportunities).

- Approach this as a critical cultural shift, not as a firefighting exercise.
- Plan and act for the long term, however much stress you may presently be under.

- Before you can do anything to improve customer relations and payments, you will need to get internal alignment.
- Mine the data you acquire through proactive discrepancy resolution and use it to explore ways to compete more effectively on costs and service.

8.2 Make it positive

It is very hard to "chase" payments in a positive way. Things have already gone wrong and the conversation is overdue and often tricky.

Yet the entire receivables discussion uses words like "chase", "pursue", "collect" and other terms which are of an adversarial nature.

By engaging early and often on service, terms and process, you can show that you care about your customer. The language is that of gratitude – for the business they have given you – and engagement in achieving a resolution whatever it may take.

Your objective is to eliminate the possibility of an adversarial discussion by closing any doors to error and late payment.

Your customer service staff engage early and sort out any issues in a timely and civil fashion.

Your sales team learns the value of being equipped with good data on service levels and resolved issues when face-to-face with the customer.

Over time your customers will turn to you and acknowledge the value to them of the changes you have made.

We have seen it time and time again.

8.3 Tell us how you got on

In this book, you have read about three very different business leaders who worked with the author. Between them they sell into more than 100 markets, which differ vastly and range from the world's most modern nations to some of the poorest and least developed.

Yet they have found that, though details and taxonomies vary, the principles of the VRC apply everywhere.

We love to learn and we invite you the reader to try out what we are suggesting, see how you get on, and share progress – and challenges – with us.

Part 9
Appendices

Appendix 1
Acronyms you will need

AR – Accounts Receivable

BPDSO – Best Possible DSO

DSO – Days Sales Outstanding

IDM – Integrated Discrepancy Management

KYC – Know Your Customer

LRF – Lost Revenue Factor

TCS – Total Cost to Serve

VRC – Virtuous Revenue Cycle

Appendix 2
Credit policy template

CREDIT MANAGEMENT POLICY

XYZ Corporation

Last updated on <insert date>
by Group Accounts, XYZ Corporation

Contents

1. Set-up of the Credit Function
2. Objectives of the Credit Management Function
3. Terms and Conditions of Sale
4. Payment Terms
5. Invoicing
6. Opening of New Accounts
7. Setting Credit Limits
8. Credit Vetting
9. Credit Holds and Waivers
10. Collections Strategy
11. Discrepancy Management
12. Bad Debt and Unresolved Discrepancies

Appendices

Appendix A – Standard Terms and Conditions
Appendix B – Sample Terms Confirmation Letter
Appendix C – Tier 1 and Tier 2 Customers and Baselining Returns
Appendix D – Credit Application Form
Appendix E – Collections Intensity Matrix
Appendix F – Summary of Activities for Collections Officers and
Schedule of Daily, Weekly and Monthly Activities
Appendix G – Samples of Dunning Letters
Appendix H – Resolution and Escalation Areas, and Response Times

1. Set-up of the Credit Function

Group Accounts is responsible for the overall credit management of XYZ Corporation. Only Group Accounts can input and change the financial details of the customer, including the credit limit, in the Wilson system.

Any changes to this Credit Management Policy can only be made with the written approval of the Senior Finance Manager Peter Lim.

2. Objectives of the Credit Management Function

Credit management starts with the sale and goes right through to full and final payment. It is as important a part of the deal as closing the sale. It is about minimizing the time and effort spent on chasing up unpaid invoices and ensuring that resources expanded on credit management are efficiently used.

Effective credit management minimizes XYZ's financial risk exposure and Days Sales Outstanding (DSO), while supporting XYZ's efforts to increase sales, margins and financial returns.

3. Terms and Conditions of Sale

All sales are to be subject to XYZ Corporation's Standard Terms and Conditions and acknowledged by the customer in writing.

Any non-standard terms offered (except for the payment term), including tenders that request conditions that contradict, deviate from or do not recognize XYZ Corporation's standard terms and conditions, should be vetted by Commercial Manager <insert name>.

XYZ Corporation's Standard Terms and Conditions of sale are attached in Appendix A.

4. Payment Terms

XYZ Corporation's standard payment term as specified in the Standard Terms and Conditions of sale is 30 days net from the date of the invoice. A terms confirmation letter should be sent to each customer to confirm in writing the agreed payment terms. A sample of XYZ Corporation's terms confirmation letter is attached in Appendix B.

Any deviation from the standard payment term should be referred to Senior Finance Manager Peter Lim for approval. A non-standard payment term may only apply for up to 12 months at a time. Group Accounts should review the non-standard payment term prior to its expiry to determine if it should continue to apply. If the non-standard payment term is not reviewed prior to its expiry date, the payment term for the customer will automatically revert to the standard payment term of 30 days net from invoice date.

The non-standard payment term should be communicated to the customer in writing by the sales rep. The customer's written acknowledgement of the term and expiration should be obtained, and a copy of it given to Group Accounts.

XYZ Corporation's list of Tier 1 and Tier 2 customers, and the terms baselining returns for customers in Singapore, is attached in Appendix C.

5. Invoicing
Customers on agreements with regular invoicing arrangements should be invoiced as specified in the agreements. Direct charge customers and customers on agreements with non-regular invoicing arrangements should be invoiced immediately upon shipment of products or completion of service.

6. Opening of New Accounts
To limit credit risk, it is important that during customer master file set-up, information must be accurate and complete. Ensure that there are no duplicate codes for the same debtor and all administration details of the new accounts are accurately documented and recorded.

A Credit Application Form should accompany every request for the opening of a new customer account. It serves as an information gathering and assessment tool to determine the credit limit and payment term, and is a legal document that binds the customer to XYZ Corporation's terms and conditions. XYZ's sales rep should forward the customer's signed Credit Application Form to Customer Service <Accounts Receivable?> for entering into the customer master file.

XYZ Corporation's Credit Application Form is attached in Appendix D.

The customer is required to provide at least one bank reference and three trade references on its credit application. Ask for trade references where the customer has had trade dealings for at least one to two years, and at least one reference should be from XYZs industry. The latter will help ascertain whether the customer has abandoned one supplier to join the other due to payment or credit limit problems.

Thorough credit reference checks should be conducted for applicants which are deemed to be Tier 1 customers.

Bank references provided should be assessed based on the following guidelines:
a. Find out the value of depository and loan balances.
b. Find out whether depository and loan balances are handled as agreed.
c. Find out if there are any overdraft balances and late repayments.

Trade references provided should be assessed based on the following guidelines:
a. Find out whether the reference provided is a primary or secondary supplier to the customer. A primary supplier on which the customer's business depends tends to get paid first.
b. Find out if the references provided are related parties to avoid biased reference.
c. Find out if the customer has any special terms with the references provided.
d. Find out the customer's general payment experience with the reference, e.g., slow 30, slow 45, slow 60, satisfactory, unsatisfactory, early payment for discount, etc.
e. Ask for the duration of the customer's relationship with the reference.

7. Setting Credit Limits

A credit limit must be assigned to every customer and be regularly reviewed depending on the customer's risk category. Based on this assessment, the credit limit should reflect a level of acceptable risk to XYZ, and at the same time be able to support sales activity.

The credit limit for a customer should be calculated as follows:
Credit limit = S * (IPT + V)

where
- S Average monthly sales for the previous 12 months, or anticipated monthly sales if new customer
- IPT : Average invoice payment terms (in months)
- V: Variance to cover delayed payment and variations in order volume (in months)

XYZ Corporation will generally give the customer a variance of 45 days (i.e., 1.5 months). Therefore, based on XYZ's standard payment term of 30 days net from invoice date (i.e., 1 month), the credit limit for a customer should be 2.5 times the customer's average monthly sales, calculated as follows:

Credit limit = S * (1 + 1.5) = S * 2.5

Credit limits are always temporary and their starting date and expiry date should be registered. The credit limit periods to be assigned are as follows:

Customer Risk Category	Credit Limit Period
- New customer	6 months
- Existing customer, slow payment record	6 months
- Existing customer, satisfactory payment record	12 months

If a credit limit is not reviewed prior to its expiry date, the credit limit must automatically be set to zero and remain zero until such time that the credit limit is reviewed and approved. <feasible?>

Note that credit limits reflect only the invoice total on the account. They do not reflect committed orders, work in progress or uninvoiced products or services.

The value of any legitimate disputes should also be removed from the credit limit calculation.

8. Credit Vetting

Credit vetting should be conducted thoroughly and on a regular basis. Credit vetting for new customers should take place before contract signature or order entry, whichever is earlier. Existing customers should be vetted at least annually. In addition, Tier 1 customers are required to provide copies of their latest annual financial statements. (See section on Setting Credit Limits for credit limit periods.)

Credit vetting should also be conducted when:
- the customer's monthly sales rapidly increases or decreases;
- the management of the customer's company changes; or adverse reports on the customer's credit worthiness are received through sales, media, other suppliers, etc.

XYZ's sales reps are the direct source of information on the credit worthiness of customers. The credit management system is dependent on the quality and dependability of this information. Sales representatives should feedback to Group Accounts immediately any relevant information on the financial stability of the customer. Credit vetting alone is no substitute for proactive account management.

9. Credit Holds and Waivers

A new order by a customer will go on credit hold if:
- the invoice total on the customer's account has exceeded the credit limit assigned to the customer; or there is any undisputed balance in the customer's account that is more than 90 days past due.

A customer on credit hold is viewed as temporarily "less than creditworthy" until the conditions for order release are met. These usually include payment of all or part of the outstanding balance in order that the amount outstanding falls below the credit limit.

In cases where XYZ could potentially be found liable for causing damage or injury to the customer due to the non-supply of product/service, XYZ may require the customer to pay cash in advance to ensure continued supply of product/service until such time the conditions for order release are met.

Credit hold will not apply if non-payment is due to legitimate disputes, i.e., discrepancies which require resolution on the part of XYZ. Unpaid invoices which are not specifically disputed should be included in the calculation of the credit limit, notwithstanding that the customer has refused to pay on account of disputes on other invoices.

10. Collections Strategy

Accounts Receivable is responsible for ensuring that cash is collected on outstanding invoices on or before the date it is due to XYZ.

The collections strategy, which is differentiated according to customer tiers, is focused on proactive account management. It enhances the order-to-cash process through more effective collection of accounts receivable, thereby improving credit management and reducing Days Sales Outstanding.

Customers	Collections Strategy	Timing
Tier 1	Proactive service calls	I+10 days
	Proactive courtesy calls	T-7 days
	Reminder calls	T+3, T+30 and T+60 days
Tier 2	Reminder calls	T+3, T+30 and T+60 days
Tier 3	Dunning letters	T+30, T+45 and T+60 days
High Risk Accounts	Proactive calls	Selective proactive contact
All	Pre-Collections Agency Referral call and letter	T+90 days

Note: I refers to the date of the invoice. | T refers to the date the invoice is due for payment.

High Risk Accounts are identified on a case-by-case basis by Group Accounts
Manager Manuel Papoulias based on the specific characteristics of or adverse
changes to their risk profiles.

All customers with outstanding balances which are more than 90 days overdue
should receive a pre-collections agency referral call and letter at least 10 days
before the referral is made to a XYZ nominated debt collections agency.

XYZ Corporation's collections intensity matrix for the different customer
segments is attached in Appendix E.

The summary of activities for XYZ Corporation's collections officers, and their
schedule of daily, weekly and monthly activities are attached in Appendix F.

Samples of dunning letters and pre-collections agency referral letter for XYZ
Corporation are attached in Appendix G.

In addition, Customer Service will make proactive service calls to Tier 1 customers
10 days after the goods are shipped (and the invoice issued) to confirm order
receipt, enquire about product and service satisfaction and confirm invoice
accuracy. A key objective of the call is to identify unmet customer expectations or
discrepancies that may prevent on-time collection well before the invoice is due,
providing sufficient time for resolution and on-time payment.

11. Discrepancy Management
Any unmet customer expectations (or discrepancies) that may prevent the
collection of accounts receivable should be identified and resolved as early as
possible so that the collection of cash is not delayed.

Discrepancies identified should be referred to the appropriate functional area for
resolution, and the expected resolution date communicated accordingly.

XYZ Corporation's discrepancy management resolution and escalation areas, and
the corresponding response times are attached in Appendix H.

Discrepancies which are not resolved by the expected resolution date will be escalated to the pre-defined escalation area. Any discrepancies that remain unresolved after the expected response time will be further escalated to the final escalation area.

12. Bad Debt and Unresolved Discrepancies

Bad debt should be managed by Group Accounts in accordance with Generally Accepted Accounting Principles <or is it IAS?> and with XYZ Corporation's accounting policy. In the event of liquidation, administration, receivership, confirmed permanent closure of a business, etc., Group Accounts will pursue all avenues of recovery up to and beyond the bad debt write-off.

Discrepancies which remain unresolved after final escalations are the joint responsibility of Country Director Steve Yao and Group Accounts. They should be reviewed regularly and a decision should be taken on the appropriate course of action. Such action could include negotiating a discount with the customer, writing off small disputed items or crediting the larger disputed items.

Appendix A – Standard Terms and Conditions

Last updated on <insert date>.

Appendix B – Sample Terms Confirmation Letter

Dear <customer name>,

As detailed in XYZ's Standard Terms & Conditions disclosure and printed on all our invoices, XYZ offers its customers standard credit terms of 30 days from invoice date. Your company has been sent this letter because our records show your past payment performance has not met the stated terms.

We would like to reiterate that your payment terms with XYZ are 30 days from invoice date – which means we expect to be able to cash the payment on the 30th day after the invoice date, the latest. We kindly ask that you amend your internal payment processes to meet this obligation.

If you currently have a written agreement with XYZ containing alternate payment terms, please make the change on the attached form and return it to the above address together with a copy of the written agreement. We would like your response sent back to us by Monday, 5 December.

Please do not hesitate to contact the undersigned should you wish further clarification on this issue. Thank you for your attention to this matter and we look forward to continuing the supplier relationship that we currently enjoy.

Best Regards,

District Manager

Last updated on <insert date>.

Appendix C – Tier 1 and Tier 2 Customers and Baselining Returns

Last updated on 11 Nov 2020

Appendix D – Credit Application Form

Last updated on 11 Nov 2020

Appendix E – Collections Intensity Matrix

Last updated on 11 Nov 2020

**Appendix F – Summary of Activities for Collections Officers
and Schedule of Daily, Weekly and Monthly Activities**

Last updated on 11 Nov 2020

Appendix G – Samples of Dunning Letters

Last updated on 11 Nov 2020

page 12

Appendix H – Resolution and Escalation Areas, and Response Times

Discrepancy Type	Resolution Area	Response Time (days)	1st Escalation Area	Response Time (days)	Final Escalation Area
Wrong product invoiced	CS	4	Site Mgr	10	Country Dir / BU Head
Wrong product delivered	CS	4	Site Mgr	10	Country Dir / BU Head
Wrong PO Number	CS	4	Site Mgr	10	Country Dir / BU Head
Expired PO Number	CA	4	Site Mgr	10	Country Dir / BU Head
Missing PO Number	S	4	District Mgr	10	Country Dir / BU Head
Wrong price	S	7	District Mgr	10	Country Dir / BU Head
Price increase disputed by customer	S	7	District Mgr	10	Country Dir / BU Head
Terms Not Agreed	S.	7	District Mgr	10	Country Dir / BU Head
Customer has no funds	S	4	District Mgr	10	Country Dir / BU Head
Duplicate Invoice	CS	4	Site Mgr	10	Country Dir / BU Head
Wrong Site	CS	4	Site Mgr	10	Country Dir / BU Head
Wrong part number/pack size	CS	4	Site Mgr	10	Country Dir / BU Head
Late / delayed delivery	CS	4	Site Mgr	10	Country Dir / BU Head
No Proof of Delivery	CS	4	Site Mgr	10	Country Dir / BU Head
No service report	S	4	District Mgr	10	Country Dir / BU Head
Fuel surcharge not agreed/disputed	S	7	District Mgr	10	Country Dir / BU Head

Credit application/agreement template

CREDIT APPLICATION/AGREEMENT

TERMS ARE NETT CASH 30 DAYS FROM INVOICE DATE EXCEPT CASH SALES ACCOUNTS ALL SALES ARE SUBJECT TO XYZ CORPORATION'S STANDARD TERMS AND CONDITIONS

CUSTOMER INFORMATION

Legal Business Name:				
Business/Trading Name:			ABN:	
Phone No:		Fax No:	Email:	
Postal Address:				
		Postcode:	Website:	
Invoicing Preference:	☐ **Mail**	☐ **Fax**	☐ **Email**	

Type of Business: ☐ Corporation ☐ State / Govt ☐ Partnership ☐ Sole Proprietor			
Business Activity:		Years this business Established:	
Annual Dollar Sales:		Financial Statements: ☐ Enclosed	☐ Not Enclosed

Director(s) / Owner(s)		
1. Name:	Title:	
2. Name:	Title:	

Delivery Address:		
		Postcode:
Contact Name:	Title:	
(preferably person who authorizes purchases)	Phone No:	Email:

Anticipated Dollar Purchase per Month:		
Accounts Payable Contact:	Phone No:	Email:

BANK REFERENCES

1. Bank Name:		Branch:
Phone No:	Fax No:	Account Officer:
Address:		
		Postcode:
Checking A/C No:	Savings A/C No:	Loan No:

2. Bank Name:		Branch:
Phone No:	Fax No:	Account Officer:
Address:		
		Postcode:
Checking A/C No:	Savings A/C No:	Loan No:

PLEASE TURN OVER

TRADE REFERENCES

1. Company Name:		Account No:
Contact Name:	Phone No:	Fax No:
Address:		
		Postcode:
No. of years done business with this Company:		

2. Company Name:		Account No:
Contact Name:	Phone No:	Fax No:
Address:		
		Postcode:
No. of years done business with this Company:		

3. Company Name:		Account No:
Contact:	Phone No:	Fax No:
Address:		
		Postcode:
No. of years done business with this Company:		

In signing this Credit Application/Agreement, the Customer hereby grants permission for credit information to be verified by the companies and financial institutions that the Custome has specified on this document and others that XYZ Corporation becomes aware of during the credit review process and from time to time.

In order for XYZ Corporation to sell and to continue to sell to the Customer, the Customer hereby represents and warrants that it is solvent and that it pays its obligations as they become due.

Faxed documents will be deemed as original. No oral agreements will be accepted. The terms on this Credit Application/ Agreement overrides all others.

Company Name: _____

Authorized Signature: _____   **Date:** _____

Signatory Name (pls. print): _____   **Title:** _____

Please Fax the completed document to <insert fax no.>
Or Mail it to

Or contact Accounts Receivable at <insert phone no.> if you have any queries.
This application must be completed in full in order to be processed.

For XYZ Corporation's Use Only

Credit References Checked: ☐ Yes ☐ No		
Comments:		
Credit Amount Requested:	Credit Amount Approved:	Sales Rep:
Applicant: ☐ New ☐ Existing, being renewed	☐ Existing, requesting increase in credit limit	

Appendix 3
Proactive collections, guidelines, script

Appendix 3 - PROACTIVE CALLING SIGNALS INTENTION TO ENHANCE CUSTOMER SERVICE

Taking the time to investigate and resolve issues proactively will encourage the customers to pay on time – "If you don't care why should they?"

This approach will result in an overall increase in customer satisfaction, which is a significant factor in getting customers to pay on time

The **first proactive call** to each customer is extremely important. It will **determine how receptive** the customer will be to future proactive calls.

Appendix 3 - PROFILE FOR CUSTOMER SERVICE OFFICER

Minimum Requirements

Education: University graduate or equivalent
Personality: Outgoing, good communication and interpersonal skills, customer oriented with excellent servicing attitude
Experience: Previous exposure to customer contacts preferred, 3-4 years relevant working experience
Specific knowledge: Good English and Mandarin. Literacy in Microsoft Word, Excel, knowledge of SAP an advantage

Main Tasks

1. Customer Contact

Maintain high service levels for top tier customer accounts. Initiate contact with these customers, collect customer demands and proactive order taking. Visit top tier customers regularly to maintain good relationships.

Work as the first contact point for customer inquiries. Respond to customer inquiries about order status, delivery status, invoice items, etc.

Act as primary point of customer contact for all service-related issues. Collect information on customer's problems and record them in the Dispute Management tool. Coordinate with sales, logistics. warehouse, finance and service providers to solve problems and take the necessary corrective actions.

Proactively follow-up with top tier customer accounts after completion of orders

Appendix 3 - THE COLLECTORS INTRODUCE THE PROACTIVE COLLECTIONS PROCESS TO TIER 1 CUSTOMERS' ACCOUNTS PAYABLE DEPARTMENT AND EXPLAIN WHY CUSTOMERS WILL BE CONTACTED BEFORE INVOICES ARE DUE

Purpose of Call

"I'm calling to let you know about our enhanced customer service program."

"As part of this program, our customer service representative will be contacting your site manager/engineer/procurement manager approximately 10 days after an order is shipped to ensure that the order was complete and correct, and identify any product or service problems as early as possible."

"Another important change is that I will be contacting you more regularly to ensure that our invoices are accurate and are scheduled for on-time payment."

"If a problem is identified, I'll work within our organization to make sure the problem is addressed timely, and I'll get back to you regularly to update you on the resolution status."

Appendix 3 - CUSTOMER SERVICE NOW REGULARLY ASKS TIER 1 CUSTOMERS SERVICE AND INVOICE RELATED QUESTIONS TO IDENTIFY CUSTOMER PROBLEMS AND ENSURE INVOICE ACCURACY

"Your product was shipped / Your service was performed on <date>."

"Is everything alright with the product / service?"

"Our invoice was issued on the same day. Have you received it?"

"Is the invoice OK to pay?"

"Who authorizes invoice payments? When will this be done?"

"Why do you think the invoice is incorrect?"

"What amount of the invoice are you disputing?"

Call objective is to motivate customer to **approve invoice for payment** if no discrepancies are identified

Appendix 3 - THE COLLECTORS NOW REGULARLY CONVEY TO CUSTOMERS THE IMPORTANCE THE COMPANY PLACES ON CREDIT TERMS AND ON-TIME PAYMENT

Educating Customer on Payment terms

"I have confirmed with my Sales Rep that the agreed payment terms between <Customer> and XYZ is 30 days net from date of the invoice."

"That means we expect to be able to cash the payment on the 30th day after invoice date, the latest."

"Credit terms are a critical part of the agreement between our companies and on-time payment is a high priority for XYZ."

"How can I assist you to ensure that XYZ is paid according to the agreed upon terms?"

Call objective is to educate the customer on payment terms and **obtain a payment promise within terms** if no discrepancies are identified

Appendix 3 - SUMMARY OF ACTIVITIES FOR COLLECTIONS OFFICER

ACTIVITY	CUSTOMER TIER	FREQUENCY	ESTIMATED TIME SPENT
Cash Allocation - Process EFT and cheque payments received - Apply EFT/cheque payments in accordance with the cash allocation process	All	Daily	2 hours

Proactive and Reminder Calls for Tier 1 Customers
- Open *Invoice Tracking Management Query*
- Filter by Tier 1 customers (~120 debtors)
- Select debtor
- Check correspondence, invoice and discrepancy status
- Follow up on discrepancy (if needed) and update Discrepancy Management log
- Telephone customer to:
  * Discuss discrepancy status (if appropriate)
  * Determine whether there are other discrepancies on outstanding invoices
  * Reiterate payment terms
  * Obtain payment promise on invoices falling due in next 7 days
    - *Proactive Courtesy Call*
  * Remind customer of overdue invoices and obtain payment promise
    - *1st Reminder Call*
    - *2nd Reminder Call*
    - *Final Notice Call*
  - Log correspondence and discrepancies (if any)
	Tier 1	Daily
		
		Refer to Collections Calls Roster
			15 mins per debtor
			
			Customers may have multiple debtor nos.

Reminder Calls for Tier 2 Customers
Open *Invoice Tracking Management Query*
Filter by Tier 2 customers (~200 debtors)
Select debtor
Check correspondence, invoice and discrepancy status
Follow up on discrepancy (if needed) and update Discrepancy Management log
Telephone customer to:
* Check whether there are any discrepancies on outstanding invoices
* Reiterate payment terms
* Remind customer of overdue invoices and obtain payment promise
  - *1st Reminder Call*
  - *2nd Reminder Call*
  - *Final Notice Call*
Log correspondence and discrepancies (if any)
	Tier 2	Daily	10-15 mins per debtor
			
			Customers may have multiple debtor nos.

Reminder Letters for T3 Customers
Open *Invoice Tracking Management Query*
Filter by Tier 3 customers
Select debtors and invoices without discrepancies
Prepare dunning letters and send to debtor:
  - *1st Reminder Letter*
  - *2nd Reminder Letter*
  - *Final Notice Letter*
	Tier 3	1x / week	30 minutes

First Escalations Open Discrepancy Management Query Filter by Discrepancy Identifier Filter by Escalation Due - Yes Check discrepancy status Escalate to First Escalation Area in one consolidated email	All	2x / week	1 hour
Final Escalations Open Discrepancy Management Query Filter by Discrepancy Identifier Filter by Final Escalation Due - Yes Check discrepancy status Escalate to Final Escalation Area in one consolidated email	Tier 1	1x / week	1 hour
Debtor Statement / Account Reconciliation Check and rectify any misallocations of cash Ensure credit notes correctly issued	Tier 2	1x / week	4 hours *Done by one collector*
Others Prepare debtor roll over Prepare monthly reports – A/R report for DM/DA/AM and for NZ Refer problem accounts to debt collectors	Tier 3	1x / week	2 hours

Appendix 3 - COLLECTIONS OFFICERS' DAILY, WEEKLY & MONTHLY ACTIVITI[ES]

		WEEK 1					WEEK 2			
	MON	TUES	WED	THURS	FRI	MON	TUES	WED	THURS	FRI
DAILY	Cash Allocation - processing of cheques and EFTs									
	Proactive and Reminder Calls for Tier 1 Customers - *Refer to Collections Calls Roster*									
	Reminder Calls for Tier 2 Customers									
	Identify account problems									
WEEKLY	1st Escalations	Reminder Letters for Tier 3 Customers	1st Escalations		Debtor Statement / Account Reconciliation[1]	1st Escalations	Reminder Letters for Tier 3 Customers	1st Escalations		Debtor Statemen[t] Account Reconciliati[on]
	Final Escalations					Final Escalations				
MONTHLY	Prepare debtor roll over[2]									
	Prepare monthly reports - A/R reports for DM/ DA/ AM[3]									

		WEEK 3					WEEK 4			
	MON	TUES	WED	THURS	FRI	MON	TUES	WED	THURS	FRI
DAILY	Cash Allocation - processing of cheques and EFTs									
	Proactive and Reminder Calls for Tier 1 Customers - *Refer to Collections Calls Roster*									
	Reminder Calls for Tier 2 Customers									
	Identify account problems									
WEEKLY	1st Escalations	Reminder Letters for Tier 3 Customers	1st Escalations		Debtor Statement / Account Reconciliation[1]	1st Escalations	Reminder Letters for Tier 3 Customers	1st Escalations		Debtor Statemen[t] Accoun[t] Reconciliat[ion]
	Final Escalations					Final Escalations				
MONTHLY										Refer prob[lem] accounts to collecto[rs]

Notes:
1 - to be done by one collector only
2 - First Monday of the month
3 - Last Friday of the month

Appendix 3 -
FIRST REMINDER LETTER –
TO BE SENT AT T+30 DAYS

\<date\>

Debtor Name	\<	\>
Debtor No.	\<	\>
Fax No.	\<	\>
Email address	\<	\>

Attention: Accounts Payable

Dear Sir / Madam

RE: FIRST REMINDER – OVERDUE ACCOUNT \$_____

We are writing to call your attention to the following overdue invoice(s):

Invoice no.	Invoice Due Date	Overdue Amt (\$)
\<insert\>	\<insert\>	\<insert\>
\<insert\>	\<insert\>	\<insert\>

As you are aware, our payment terms are 30 days net from invoice date. We are therefore eagerly awaiting your payment.

If you wish to discuss any issues, please call the undersigned immediately. Otherwise, we look forward to getting paid at the earliest.

Please ensure that payment of \$_____ reaches us by \<one week from date of letter\> at the latest.

Thank you for your business, and we anticipate your prompt response.

Please disregard this letter if you have made payment in the last few days.

Yours sincerely

\<Name\>
\<Titlte\>
\<Phone no.\>

Appendix 3 -
SECOND REMINDER
LETTER – TO BE SENT AT
T+45 DAYS

<date>

Debtor Name   <   >
Debtor No.   <   >
Fax No.   <   >
Email address   <   >

Attention: Accounts Payable

Dear Sir / Madam

RE: SECOND REMINDER – OVERDUE ACCOUNT $_____

We refer to our letter dated <insert date> in which we drew your attention to the following overdue invoice(s):

Invoice no.	Invoice Due Date	Overdue Amt ($)
<insert>	<insert>	<insert>
<insert>	<insert>	<insert>

We have to date not heard back from you on your overdue account.

We would remind you that our payment terms are 30 days net from invoice date. Please ensure that payment of $_____ reaches us immediately.

We value our business partnership and look forward to your immediate response.

Please disregard this letter if you have made payment in the last few days.

Yours sincerely

<Name>
<Titlte>
<Phone no.>

**Appendix 3 -
FINAL NOTICE LETTER –
TO BE SENT AT T+60 DAYS**

<date>

Debtor Name   <   >
Debtor No.   <   >
Fax No.   <   >
Email address   <   >

Attention: Accounts Payable

Dear Sir / Madam

RE: FINAL NOTICE – OVERDUE ACCOUNT $_____

We recently drew your attention to the following overdue invoice(s) via our letter dated <insert date>:

Invoice no.	Invoice Due Date	Outstanding Amt ($)
<insert>	<insert>	<insert>
<insert>	<insert>	<insert>

The amount of $_____ is now considerably past due.

We must receive payment immediately to keep your credit in good standing with us.

Your urgent attention is sought on this matter. Please ensure that your payment is on its way to us that there is no disruption to our business partnership.

Please disregard this letter if payment has been made in the last few days.

Yours sincerely

<Name>
<Titlte>
<Phone no.>

cc: Debtor's higher level

Appendiex 3 -
PRE-COLLECTIONS AGENCY
REFERRAL LETTER –
TO BE SENT AT T+90 DAYS

<date>

Debtor Name   <   >
Debtor No.   <   >
Fax No.   <   >
Email address   <   >

Attention: Accounts Payable

Dear Sir / Madam

RE: SERIOUSLY OVERDUE ACCOUNT $_____

We have given you more than ample time and notice regarding the following seriously overdue invoice(s):

Invoice no.	Invoice Due Date	Outstanding Amt ($)
<insert>	<insert>	<insert>
<insert>	<insert>	<insert>

We hereby put you on notice that unless we receive the amount of $_____ by <insert date>, our normal policy is to pass on such delinquent accounts to a third party collections agency or our legal counsel.

This could further jeopardize your credit rating in the industry. We trust that this will not be necessary.

Please disregard this letter if payment has been made in the last few days.

Yours sincerely

<Name>
<Titlte>
<Phone no.>

cc: Debtor's higher level

Appendix 4
Issue resolution templates

ppendix 4 - SUGGESTED CAPABILITIES FOR AN EFFECTIVE IDM WORKFLOW TOOL

FUNCTIONALITY	RATIONALE	OPTION 1	OPTION 2	OPTION 3
Multi-point issue Capture	Ability to record issue raised by internal and external customers wherever and whenever identified	Yes, if connectivity available	Yes, if connectivity available	No - version control issues because not live
Link in to invoicing system	Can draw updated invoicing data, customer data etc.	Not currently linked - would need reconfiguration	Yes	No
Automatic field population	Reduce need for manual data entry	Not currently linked - would need reconfiguration	Yes	No
Pre-assigned Issue Type	Categorise issue based on type. Enables issue to be routed based on type, customer etc. to correct resolution area. Ensures common issue types across business and enables meaningful performance reporting	Need to add drop down boxes and build performance reports	Yes	Can do issue categorisation but automated routing is difficult
Pre-assigned Resolution Area	Pre-assign Supply Chain, Finance, Accounting, R&D, sales etc. as the agreed functional area to resolve the assigned issue	Cannot pre-assign - Coordinator has to assign	Yes	Yes but automated routing is difficult
Pre-assign Time Frame	Assign specific time frame (which must be agreed by the parties involved in issue resolution) for every issue type so that issue performance can tracked	Yes	Yes	Yes
Escalation Time Capability	Pre-defined escalation areas per issue allow automatic escalation to pre-agreed areas and alert management attention for the unresolved issue	Yes	Yes	No (escalation cannot be automated)
Escalation Time Frame	Assign specific time frame (which must be agreed by the parties involved in issue resolution) for every issue type so that issue performance can be tracked	Yes	Yes	Yes (but difficult to track/automate)
Reporting	Provide reporting capability	Yes	Yes	Yes

Appendix 4 - AN EFFECTIVE DISCREPANCY TRACKING REPORT MIGHT LOOK SOMETHING LIKE THIS (RECENT CLIENT EXAMPLE)

WELCOME JOHN DOE

INVOICE TRACKING MANAGEMENT QUERY EXIT

Callout: Discrepancy details readily available

DEBTOR DETAILS	DEBTOR NUMBERS	GROUP DEBTOR	TIER	INVOICE NUMBER	INVOICE DETAILS	DUE BALANCE	INVOICE DUE DATE	DAYS OVERDUE	CORR. DETAILS	CORR. NOW DUE	CORR. DUE	CORR. LOG	DISCR. RAISED	DISCR. STATUS	DISCR. LOG
VIEW	2AM246		1	694269	VIEW	$1,186.85	01-Dec-20	-23	NONE	NONE	NO	LOG	NO		LOG
VIEW	2AM246		1	689647	VIEW	$1,169.30	02-Nov-20	6	NONE	FRST RMD	YES	LOG	NO		LOG
VIEW	2AM249			108	VIEW	$3,145.07	03-Dec-20	-25	NONE	NONE	NO	LOG	NO		LOG
VIEW	2AM249			978	VIEW	$2,100.09	21-Aug-20	79	NONE	FNL NTC	YES	LOG	YES	ASSIGNED	LOG
VIEW	2AM249			681032	VIEW	$595.90	04-Sep-20	65	NONE	FNL NTC	YES	LOG	YES	ASSIGNED	LOG
VIEW	2AM249		1	684572	VIEW	$595.90	01-Oct-20	38	NONE	SCND RMD	YES	LOG	YES	ASSK NED	LOG
VIEW	2AM249		1	689461	VIEW	$10,520.40	02-Nov-20	6	NONE	FRST RMD		LOG			LOG
VIEW	2AM249		1	694085	VIEW	$10,678.2?		23	NONE			LOG	N		LOG
VIEW	2AM253		1	689665	VIEW	$1,232.00		6	NONE			LOG	N		LOG
VIEW	2AM253		1	694279	VIEW	$1,250.48		-23	NONE			LOG	NO		LOG
VIEW	2AM255		1	694593	VIEW	$289.08	01-Dec-20	-23	NONE	NONE	NO	LOG	NO		LOG
VIEW	2AM255		1	689980	VIEW	$289.08	02-Nov-20	6	NONE	FRST RMD	YES	LOG	NO		LOG
VIEW	2AN330		1	693680	VIEW	$61,532.24	30-Nov-20	-22	NONE	NONE	NO	LOG	NO		LOG
VIEW	2AN330		1	693216	VIEW	$3,685.00	26-Nov-20	-18	NONE	SRVC CLL	YES	LOG	NO		LOG
VIEW	2AN330		1	683923	VIEW	$418.00	20-Nov-20	-12	SRVC CLL	SRVC CLL	NO	VIEW	NO		VIEW
VIEW	2AN330		1	683925	VIEW	$572.00	20-Nov-20	-12	NONE	SRVC CLL	NO	VIEW	NO		VIEW
VIEW	2AN330		1	691168	VIEW	$357,843.20	28-Nov-20	-20	NONE	SRVC CLL	YES	VIEW	NO		VIEW
VIEW	2AN330		1	695051	VIEW	$5,940.00	03-Dec-20	-25	NONE	NONE	NO	VIEW	NO		VIEW
VIEW	2AN330		1	695307	VIEW	$6,490.00	04-Dec-20	-26	NONE	NONE	NO	VIEW	NO		VIEW

Callouts: "Debtor credit limit and contact details"; "Provides invoice balance, due date and days overdue"; "Prompts correspondence and captures call details"; "Flags accounts with discrepancies and shows current status"

TOTAL INVOICE VALUE $8,553,859.62 TOTAL NO INVOICES 1089

Appendix 4 - AN OVERDUE DISCREPANCY TRACKING REPORT MIGHT LOOK SOMETHING LIKE THIS (RECENT CLIENT EXAMPLE)

WELCOME JOHN DOE

DISCREPANCY MANAGEMENT QUERY EXIT

VIEW/EDIT	CASE NO.	DEBTOR NO.	DISPUTED AMOUNT	TOTAL INVOICE BALANCE DUE	DISCREPANCY IDENTIFIER	DISCR. STATUS	AREA ASSIGNED	ASSIGNEE NAME	DAYS SINCE ASSN	E SC. DUE	DISCR. RAISED	AGRD PYMNT DATE	AGRD PYMNT DATE
VIEW	406	6WE200	$2,020.10	$2,020.10	David Bell	ASSIGNED	Richard Webb	Richard Webb	15	NO	NO		
VIEW	407	6WO400	$37,828.30	$37,828.30	David Bell	ASSIGNED	Richard Webb	Adriana Gallo	15	NO	NO		
VIEW	408	6WO401	$1,408.0?	$1,408.0?	David Bell	ASSIGNED	Richard Webb	Adriana Gallo	15	NO	NO		
VIEW	409			$62.7?		ASSIGNED	Sales	Mark Landstra	5	NO	NO		
VIEW	410			$595.9?		ASSIGNED	Sales	Mark Landstra	6				
VIEW	411			$405.90		ASSIGNED	Customer Service	Jill Fitzgerald	15				
VIEW	412	2AM249	$10,520.40	$10,520.40	Anthony Skoulos	ASSIGNED	Sales	Eric Sinco	15				
VIEW	413	2AM249	$10,678.21	$10,678.21	Anthony Skoulos	ASSIGNED	Sales	Richard Nijoff	15	YES	NO		
VIEW	414	2AM253	$1,232.00	$1,232.00	Anthony Skoulos	ASSIGNED	Sales	Ron Corcoran	15	YES	NO		
VIEW	415	2AM253	$1,250.48	$1,250.48	Jerry Zissis	ASSIGNED	Sales	Richard Silvak	15	YES	NO		
VIEW	416	2AM255	$289.08	$1,000,801.00	Jerry Zissis	ASSIGNED	Sales	Tom Silvak	15	YES	NO		
VIEW	417	2AM255	$3,222.00	$63,360.28	Anthony Skoulos	ASSIGNED	Sales	Jill Fitzgerald	15	YES	NO		
VIEW	418	3DE875	$354.20	$61,387.42	Anthony Skoulos	ASSIGNED	Sales	Steve Anello	15	YES	NO		
VIEW	420	2AM249	$3,145.74	$2,1000.00	Anthony Skoulos	ASSIGNED	Customer Service	Justin Wallace	15	YES	NO		
VIEW	422	2AM249	$10,520.40	$11,712.00	Jerry Zissiz	ASSIGNED	Sales	Justin Wallace	14	YES	NO		
VIEW	452	3NE201	$338.58	$338.58	David Bell	ASSIGNED	Customer Service	Bob Baker	14	YES	NO		
VIEW	454	3NE208	$207.35	$357,843.20	David Bell	ASSIGNED	Sales	Bob Baker	14	YES	NO		
VIEW	456	2AN330	$1,358.74	$751.54	Anthoy Skoulos	ASSIGNED	Sales	Ana Greenfield	14	YES	NO		
VIEW	457	3JA723	$267.30	$692.05	Jerry Zissis	ASSIGNED	Customer Service	George Wallis	14	YES	NO		

Callouts: "Discrepancies are assigned a unique case # for tracking"; "Discrepancy amount and resolution status can easily be tracked"; "Discrepany age prompts escalation"

TOTAL VALUE $1,276,495.38 $3,227,501.00 TOTAL NUMBER OF CASES 269

Appendix 4 - SALES RELATED DISCREPANCIES ARE SENT TO REPS VIA PDF FILE, AND A SUMMARY OF OUTSTANDING DISCREPANCIES BY SALES REP WILL BE SENT WEEKLY

DEBTOR DISCREPANCY		DISCREPANCY STATUS - ASSIGNED				PDF	PRINT		EXIT

CASE NUMBER	422	TEL NO	02 9110-91115	CREDIT LIMIT	$30,000.00	DISTRICT	
DEBTOR NO	2AM249	FAX NO	02 0009-91117	TERMS	30 DAYS NETT	REP CODE	
DEBTOR NAME	ABCDE PACKAGING	EMAIL	barry.megan@abcde.com	TERMS	30 DAYS NETT	REP CODE	

IDENTIFIER	PERRY BISSIS	DISPUTED INVOICES:	INVOICE NO	INVOICE NO	INVOICE DATE	DUE DATE	DAYS OVERDUE
DATE LOGGED	24-Oct-20		681032	$595.90	5/08/2020	4/09/20	66
DISCREPANCY REASON CODE	6 — Wrong price		684572	$10,520.40	1/09/2020	1/10/20	39
DESCRIPTION	Wrong price		680461	$10,520.40	3/10/2020	2/11/20	7
DISPUTED AMT	$10,520.40		TOTAL	$21,636.70		REMOVE SELECTED INVOICE	
CURRENCY	AUS $						
DETAILS/ COMMENTS	Evan in A/P has notified that the actual amount on the invoices quoted should be $9924.50 inclusive of GST please review.						

Sales reps are provided with the information they need to resolve the discrepancy

ASSIGNED	Yes		FINAL ESC. DUE DATE: 13-Nov-05 DUE: NO
DATE	24-Oct-20		FOLLOW UP	DATE
AREA ASSIGNED	Sales		
ASSIGNEE NAME	Warren Newfield		ESCALATED	No	AREA
EXP. RES. DATE	31-Oct-20		DATE ESC.	NAME

RESOLVED	No		CREDIT NOTE ☐		CREDIT NOTE DATE
RESOLUTION OVERCOME			CREDIT NOT NO		CREDIT NOTE AMOUNT
DATE DEBTOR INFORMED		AGREED PAYMENT DATE		CLOSED	No	DATE CASH COLLECTION

Appendix 4 - TRAINING SCENARIOS FOR COLLECTIONS & DISCREPANCY MANAGEMENT TOOL

1. Plan calling schedule for the day

 a. Tier 1 and Tier 2 customers
 b. CS Service calls
 c. Collectors, Courtesy calls, 1st Reminder calls, 2nd Reminder calls, Final Notice
 d. Correspondence due - Yes
 e. Prioritise debtors

2. Make call and log correspondence

 a. Whether to make call if discrepancy has been logged against invoice
 b. Whether CS should make service call if courtesy call has been made by collector
 c. Service call for agreement invoice vs direct charge invoice

3. Log discrepanices

 a. CS - wrong product invoiced, wrong product delivered, wrong PO number, duplicate invoice, wrong site, wrong part number/pack size, late/delayed delivery, no proof of delivery
 b. CA - expired PO number
 c. Sales - missing PO number, price increase disputed, terms ot agreed, customer has no funds, no service report, fuel surcharge not agreed
 d. Assign to resolver - via email or tool

Appendix 5
Audit and measurement

Appendix 5 - SALES SUPPORT WITH CONFIRMING CREDIT TERMS, PROVIDING COMPLETE ORDER INFORMATION AND RESOLVING DISCREPANCIES TIMELY IS CRITICAL TO REDUCING DSO

DOMAIN	ACTIVITY	SUPPORTING EVIDENCE	% COMPLETE	TARGET COMPLETION DATE	RE-AUDIT DATE	COMMENTS & ACTIONS
Sales	Confirm payment terms with customers and importance of on-time payment	Check whether terms confirmation letter was sent to key customers. Discuss customer terms discrepancies with collectors				
	Assist receivable collection process when requested	Interview collectors. Review CDMS logs for sales assistance requests, and measure collection time				
	Assist collection of long O/D accounts	Interview Richard Webb, Adriana Gallo. Review long O/D collection logs				
	Take action when discrepancies are identified	Review CDMS management reports to determine % of unresolved sales discrepancies, number of required escalations and average resolution time				
	Provide accurate & complete order information to CS	Interview CS reps. Review number of discrepancies and credit notes related to order entry				
	Review order confirmations and respond to CS timely with problems or changes	Interview sales and CS reps. Review number of discrepancies and credit notes related to order entry				
	Management reports are reviewed and responded to regularly	Interview sales rep or DM to determine how often reports are received, reviewed and discussed with the group				
	Contracts / agreements renewed on-time	Review agreement renewal/expiration report. Interview Gay Thompson				

Appendix 5 - CUSTOMER SERVICE WILL BE MEASURED ON PROACTIVE SERVICE CALLS, ASSIGNING & TRACKING DISCREPANCY RESOLUTION, AND RESOLVING CS RELATED DISCREPANCIES

DOMAIN	ACTIVITY	SUPPORTING EVIDENCE	% COMPLETE	TARGET COMPLETION DATE	RE-AUDIT DATE	COMMENTS & ACTIONS
Customer Service	Enhanced customer mapping	Review customer mapping template. Discuss Tier 1 customer process understanding with proactive service personnel				
	Proactive service calls for Tier 1 customer to proactive capture issues	Interview designated CS representative & Jill Fitzgerald to determine proactive calls are made. Review call notes / discrepancies in CDMS. Calculate % customers contacted on-time, % called late and % not called				
	Escalate discrepancies when necessary	Check CDMS to determine if CS identified discrepancies were escalated when issue unresolved. Review escalation due date vs. actual escalation date				
	Resolve customer service discrepancies	Review CDMS management reports to determine % of unresolved CS discrepancies, number of required escalations and average resolution time				
	Order notification	Check with CS order entry if order notifications are sent. Review order notification template				
	Contracts / agreements renewed on-time	Review agreement renewal/expiration report. Interview Gay Thompson				

Appendix 5 - FINANCE OWNS THE PROACTIVE COLLECTIONS PROCESS AND THE IDM (1)

DOMAIN	ACTIVITY	SUPPORTING EVIDENCE	% COMPLETE	TARGET COMPLETION DATE	RE-AUDIT DATE	COMMENTS & ACTIONS
Finance	Improved proactive collections skills	Interview Manuel Papoulias to determine collector skills improvement. Monitor a sample of customer calls for adherence to scripts / best practice				
	Monitor approaching payment of T1 and T2 customers	Interview Manuel Papoulias and collectors				
	Make T1 proactive courtesy call	Interview collectors & Manuel Papoulias to determine if proactive calls are made. Review call notes / discrepancies in CDMS. Calculate % customers contacted on-time, % called late and % not called				
	Make T1 & T2 first reminder calls	Interview collectors & Manuel Papoulias to determine if first reminder calls are made. Review call notes / discrepancies in CDMS. Calculate % customers contacted on-time, % called late and % not called				
	Make T1 & T2 second reminder calls	Interview collectors & Manuel Papoulias to determine if second reminder calls are made. Review call notes / discrepancies in CDMS. Calculate % customers contacted on-time, % called late and % not called				
	Make T1 & T2 final notice call	Interview collectors & Manuel Papoulias to determine if final notice calls are made. Review call notes / discrepancies in CDMS. Calculate % customers contacted on-time, % called late and % not called				

Appendix 5 - FINANCE OWNS THE PROACTIVE COLLECTIONS PROCESS AND THE IDM (2)

DOMAIN	ACTIVITY	SUPPORTING EVIDENCE	% COMPLETE	TARGET COMPLETION DATE	RE-AUDIT DATE	COMMENTS & ACTIONS
Finance (cont'd)	Send dunning letters to T3 customers	Interview collectors & Manuel Papoulias to determine if letters sent to all delinquent T3 customers. Review sample letters and log of letters sent. Calculate % customers contacted on-time, % contacted late and % not contacted				
	Ensure on-time payment	Identify a sample of customers with overdue balances and review DCMS to determine what was done to ensure on-time payment				
	Refer non-paying accounts to outside collection agency	Interview Manuel Papoulias. Review aged debtors report and request agency referral documentation for a sample of selected accounts				
	Escalate discrepancies when necessary	Check CDMS to determine if identified discrepancies were escalated when issue unresolved. Review escalation due date vs. actual escalation date				
	Management reports are created and reviewed regularly	Interview Manuel Papoulias to determine how often reports are created, who receives the reports, how often they are discussed				
	DSO reduction	Track overall DSO performance / trend, and performance / trend of Tier 1 customers				
	Long O/D account collection	Interview Richard Webb, Adriana Gallo and Manuel Papoulias. Review long O/D collection logs and long O/D invoice payment log				

Laus Deo Semper